PIKE PLACE MARKET Recipes

130 DELICIOUS WAYS TO BRING HOME SEATTLE'S FAMOUS MARKET

Jess Thomson

Photography by Clare Barboza

WITHDRAWN

SASQUATCH BOOKS
SEATTLE

Printed in China

Published by Sasquatch Books
17 16 15 14 13 12   9 8 7 6 5 4 3 2 1

Cover design: Anna Goldstein
Cover photographs: Clare Barboza
Interior design and composition: Kate Basart/Union Pageworks
Interior photographs: Clare Barboza

Library of Congress Cataloging-in-Publication Data is available.

ISBN-13: 978-1-57061-742-3
ISBN-10: 1-57061- 742-2

Sasquatch Books
1904 Third Avenue, Suite 710
Seattle, WA 98101
(206) 467-4300
www.sasquatchbooks.com
custserv@sasquatchbooks.com

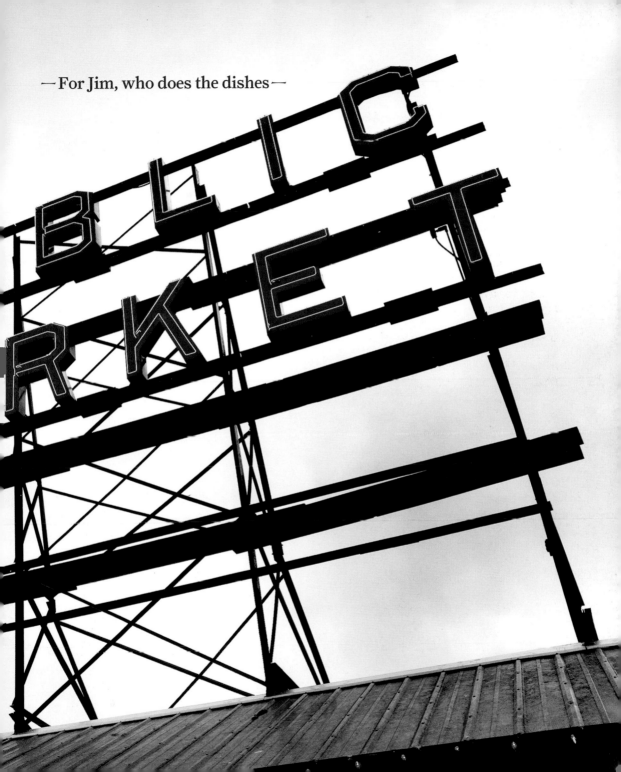

—For Jim, who does the dishes—

CONTENTS

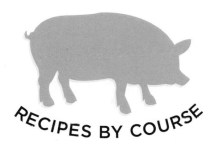

RECIPES BY COURSE

ENTRÉES

BEEF AND LAMB

FISH AND SHELLFISH

PORK

POULTRY

VEGETARIAN

SNACKS

DESSERTS

BEVERAGES

BASICS

INTRODUCTION

In 2006 I was leaning against the metal railing next to Rachel the Pig—the Pike Place Market's fund-raising mascot and certainly Seattle's most famous animal—when my phone rang. It was my husband, announcing he'd accepted a job here in the Emerald City. I jumped up, shrieked at an embarrassing volume, and gave Rachel a proud pat. I'd spent the morning wandering the Market and couldn't wait to live close enough to bring its specialties home to my own kitchen. I fantasized knowing the Market so well that I'd swoop in on a weeknight, grab just what I needed for dinner, and traipse home.

As it turns out, for a Seattleite—just like for tourists—deciding how to bring the Pike Place Market home can cause a bit of anxiety. With literally hundreds of vendors, the options are vast, and unlike at a typical grocery store, shoppers are bombarded with constantly changing inspiration. More often than not, when I pop in for, say, some fresh crab, I walk out with an olive oil I've never tried, three little paper bags filled with produce, pastries for the morning, enough cheeses for a wedding reception, and telltale crumbs on my sweater. Only occasionally do I remember the crab. But not everyone has the luxury of going back the next day, like I do.

Pike Place Market Recipes is a home cook's guide to Seattle's beloved treasure. With recipes inspired by the Market's chefs and purveyors, as well as essays that give you a behind-the-scenes view of the Market's day-to-day workings, the book is part Market companion and part bedtime story. Chefs' recipes for famous Market-area dishes, like Le Pichet's Salade Verte, Etta's Mini Dungeness Crab Cakes, and The Pink Door's Linguine alla Vongole, are a way to relive a day indulging at the Market or catch up on the places you might have missed. Original recipes from my own kitchen that use unique Market ingredients, like Spicy Marinated Feta, made with Sotto Voce's piquant olive oil, or Tart Cherry Chocolate Chunk Oatmeal Cookies, made with Chukar's dried cherries, can help you decide what to take home.

The twenty-first century has brought major changes to the Pike Place Market's food stalls. Besides celebrating its one hundredth anniversary and receiving a major structural facelift, the Market has embraced environmental awareness: Pike Place Fish, home of the world-famous fish throwers and the Market's biggest attraction, now sells only sustainable fish. More and more of the Market's produce purveyors proudly offer Washington-grown fruits and veggies, and the summer brings outdoor organic market stalls to the cobbles of Pike Place. With these changes in mind, this book is organized by where the star ingredients in each recipe come from—From the Sound focuses on seafood, for example, and From the Shops highlights recipes made with ingredients from Market retailers—to remind you that, while Pike Place Market is known as a place where you can buy almost anything almost all of the time, its restaurants and producers honor seasonality, and Seattleites are proud to acknowledge their bounty of local food.

The Pike Place Market's restaurant scene has changed also. Two of its most popular upscale restaurants, Marché (formerly Campagne) and Matt's in the Market, have been remodeled, and a third, relative newcomer Steelhead

Diner, has become a staple for locals and tourists alike. Today, favorites include dishes from Indian, Russian, Chinese, French, Italian, Japanese, Vietnamese, Spanish, British, Greek, Mediterranean, Turkish, African, Creole, and Mexican spots—and that's just lunch.

Of course, some things have stayed the same. The Athenian, the bakery-turned-seafood restaurant whose original 1909 neon sign still hangs in the Main Arcade (yes, it existed before Tom Hanks made it famous in *Sleepless in Seattle*), still feels like a gathering place. MarketSpice, the Market's first merchant, still sells its trademark tea scented with cinnamon, orange, and clove. Three Girls Bakery is still known for its sandwiches. And as before, the Market hosts handfuls of buskers every day, making every trip down Pike Place entertaining no matter what you choose to eat.

Whether you're trolling for a dinner featuring fresh halibut and the season's first Columbia River king salmon in April or shopping for holiday gifts in November, *Pike Place Market Recipes* has the inspiration you need—and with any luck, you, like the ten million other people who visit the Market each year, will be back soon, soaking up its smells and sights and feasting on its flavors. But until then, keep cooking.

MARKET HISTORY

The Pike Place Market is a raucous collision of food cultures. In the same nine-acre Historic District the Market calls home, overlooking Elliott Bay on the western edge of downtown Seattle, you can scoop up spicy lentils with spongy Ethiopian *injera* bread, tuck into high-end fish-and-chips crusted in a batter made with beer brewed right near the Market, or get Chinese dim sum to go. You'll find locals shopping for produce, visitors posing for snapshots in front of the original Starbucks store, chefs buying seafood, low-income seniors walking home to their apartments above the Market, quartets doo-wopping, and passersby gawking at the busker who does tricks with his two sweater-vested cats. Since its dedication in 1907, the Pike Place Market has been a community center. It started as a place where farmers could sell their goods directly to the consumer—hence its slogan, "Meet the Producer"—but in the century since, it's had its ups and downs, in the process becoming a Seattle icon.

The Market was built in response to a rapid rise in produce prices in the early 1900s. City councilman Thomas Revelle led an initiative to form an official public market, and on August 17, 1907, when eight farmers showed up on a rainy morning to sell produce on a newly constructed wooden plank road (now Pike Place), more than ten thousand shoppers overwhelmed them. Unlike most markets, which purchased products from farmers and then sold them to customers in turn, taking a cut of the proceeds, the Pike Place Market provided a convivial atmosphere where cooks and housewives alike could learn more about what they were buying directly from the producers, and farmers could keep the proceeds. Money from the Klondike gold rush plumped investors' wallets, and the Market's infrastructure blossomed. In the years after

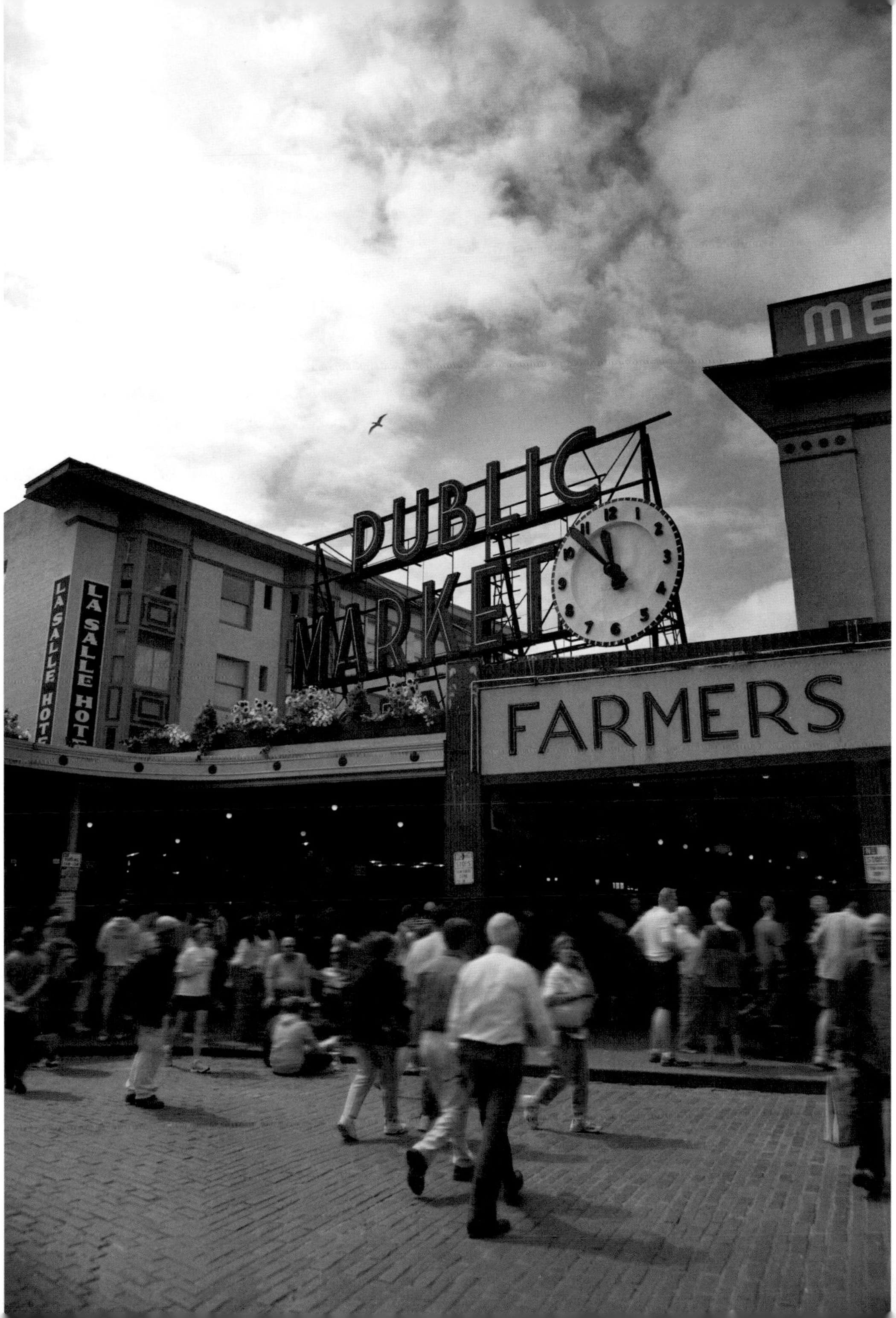
PUBLIC
MARKET
FARMERS

the Market opened, buildings were dedicated for specific purposes, and their names are still used today: the Sanitary Public Market, opened in 1910, was originally named because no horses were allowed inside. The Corner Market Building, opened in 1912, was (you guessed it) on the corner of Pike Street and First Avenue. Two years later, the main market building opened. The Economy Market Building, which was initially built to house farmers' horses but became the Market's discount section, ironically now houses DeLaurenti, a high-end specialty food market. In 1927 the Market's famous sign (the red neon clock, with the sign reading PUBLIC MARKET CENTER) was built.

Through the early part of the twentieth century—even, for the most part, during the Depression—the Market thrived, thanks in large part to the hard-working Japanese American families that formed the Market's backbone. But in February 1942 President Franklin D. Roosevelt signed Executive Order 9066 in response to the bombing of Pearl Harbor, paving the way for the nationwide internment of more than 110,000 Americans of Japanese ancestry. Many local farmers were forced to sell their property, and almost 80 percent of the Pike Place Market's producers dropped out. The Market began to collapse.

Although farmers still sold produce—many Italians took the place of the Japanese farmers—the thriving Market of the 1920s and '30s was gone. Throughout the '50s and '60s, as many downtown customers moved to suburbs, and grocery store shopping became the norm, the Market languished. The LaSalle Hotel, once belonging to Japanese owners, became a brothel, and the Market found its seedy side.

In the early 1960s a group of Seattle businessmen looking to fuel urban renewal formed the Central Business Association. Their goal was to tear the Market down and replace it with more "modern" amenities: offices, apartments, a hotel, and even a hockey rink. In 1964 Victor Steinbrueck, a University of Washington professor, started a group called Friends of the Market, which was dedicated to preserving and reinvigorating the Market, halting development, and bringing farmers back. Friends of the Market gathered twenty thousand signatures, which forced a citywide vote—and by a margin of about three to one, Seattle demanded the Market be kept.

In 1970 the state of Washington designated Pike Place Market as a Historic District, under the provisions of the National Historic Preservation Act of 1966. In 1973 the city chartered the Pike Place Market Preservation and Development Authority (PDA), which oversaw the Market's reconstruction according to its original blueprints. The PDA also manages the properties in the Historic District, coordinates farmers and retailers, and partners with the Market Foundation to support four human service agencies, which collectively help more than ten thousand people each year. Keep your eyes open, and as you walk through the Market, you'll find a medical clinic, senior center, child care and preschool, and food bank.

However, to this day, although the Pike Place Market is public, it does not receive any public money for daily operations. (In 2008 Seattle voters approved a property tax levy to fund a three-year renovation.) Other funding for the PDA comes from residential and retail rents, and the Market Foundation raises money for the Market's social services through events and ongoing contributions. The Foundation's Rachel the Pig, the famous bronze pig (and piggy bank) that stands sentry below the market's main sign, raises more than $10,000 each year.

Seattle also pitches in. In 1985, when the Market's original wooden floors were found to be rotting, the PDA started a "Pave the Market Arcade" project, where people could "buy" $35 paving tiles that had their name imprinted on them. Look down as you shop, and among the 46,500 tiles with names, you'll find the likes of Ronald Reagan—purchased by someone with absolutely no connection to the president—and some so-called celebrities, like the prime numbers from 1 to 100, near the Daily Dozen Doughnut Company.

Over the years, the way the Pike Place Market functions has changed. Today, there are eight "high stalls," or produce purveyors, so called because of the way they're elevated above the street and their produce is organized in tiers, and almost one hundred farmers rent tables by the day. Although this book focuses on its food, the Market is also home to street performers, craftspeople, and more than two hundred year-round commercial businesses, as well as the shops and restaurants immediately surrounding the official Historic District's boundaries (First Avenue to the east, Western Avenue to the west, Virginia Avenue to the north, and south of Pike Street to the south).

A cornerstone of the Market, the immigrant farming communities that sell there are also continuously evolving. In the 1980s Hmong and Mien families who had aided American soldiers during the war escaped Vietnam for fear of persecution; many found a second home at the Market's flower and vegetable stalls.

The Pike Place Market is one of the oldest continually operating public farmers' markets in the United States. It receives more than ten million visitors each year, but it's not just an icon for tourists—it's as much a working part of the Emerald City now as it was in the early twentieth century, which is why many people call it "the soul of Seattle." On a sunny summer day, when as many as thirty-five thousand people mob the Market to get a glimpse of fish flying through the air or soak up the sun in Victor Steinbrueck Park, it feels almost glamorous. But in the dead of winter, when rain drizzles down on the cobblestones, shoppers pad by with bulging totes, and the smell of fresh-baked bread infuses the air with warmth, it just feels like home.

HOW TO USE THIS BOOK

Uli Lengenberg, a German master butcher and the owner of Uli's Famous Sausage on the Market's Main Arcade, says that a recipe is a guideline. I couldn't agree more. Although the recipes in this book have been tested again and again just as they appear, please feel free to interpret them the way you wish—the magic of the Market lies in how you choose to take it home, and your shopping

experiences will inevitably be slightly different from mine.

There's a concept Uli likes to refer to that you're probably already familiar with, but that doesn't really have an English equivalent. Literally, *mit fleischeinlage* means "with a meat ingredient," but in German *einlage* has another meaning: "orthotic." Uli points to his signature giant black boots, laughing. Cooking something *mit fleischeinlage* means that you add to it what you have, and all those little things—leftovers, older vegetables, special ingredients that you have in miniscule quantities—are what add up to make a dish special. They are what *supports* the dish. As you cook, let your brain and your heart guide you. Within reason, tweak the recipes as you see fit, adding ingredients you think will support your version best. I'm sure the Market's other chefs and purveyors would concur.

Of course, certain recipes in this book call for ingredients that can only be found at the Pike Place Market—or *could* only be found there, until, on the eighth day, God created online shopping. For a full list of websites for the businesses discussed in this book—many of which are very happy to send a box across the country, or around the world, for that matter—see Resources, on page 193. Or just buy a little soft cooler at Sur La Table and get ready to argue with the airlines about your baggage allowance.

Tips

Every cook has her own kitchen, and with it come her own habits. When using this book, be sure to read the tips that are scattered throughout, which contain little tidbits of information—Market Tips address how to purchase or prepare certain ingredients, like crab or pancetta. Other notes sprinkled throughout the book tell you when you can make a recipe over the course of multiple days, or what practices I use when baking, for example. Please read every recipe thoroughly before turning on your stove!

MARKET TIPS

Asking for Help (page 73)
Buying and Cooking Salmon (page 22)
Buying Crab Legs (page 17)
Buying Spices (page 92)
Debearding Mussels (page 19)
Dressing for Dinner (page 63)
Freezing Cookie Dough (page 51)
Having Prosciutto Sliced (page 45)
My Favorite Appliance (page 75)
Peeling Pearl Onions (page 173)
Preparing a Chicken for Roasting (page 100)
Storing Mushrooms (page 33)
Toasting Nuts (page 58)
Toasting Spices (page 8)
Using Vanilla Beans (page 138)

FROM *the* SOUND

RECIPE LIST

FLYING FISH:

Redefining "Catch and Release" with a Lesson from the Boys in Orange

When you step behind the counter to catch a six-pound salmon at Pike Place Fish Market, the purveyor that's world famous for its theatrical fish-throwing antics, there's not all that much to learn. You put an apron on. You turn your left shoulder toward the fish, as if you were a batter anticipating a pitch. A guy clad in the company's signature orange rubber overalls guides your hands into place, placing the back hand higher than the front one, just like in its logo. There's some barely intelligible call-and-response shouting, then the fish swims through the air toward you, head high, and lands snugly between the thumb and forefinger of each of your outstretched hands. You've clearly missed your calling in life.

"Everything we do here is learnable and teachable," says Taho Kakutani, a bright-eyed fishmonger who's been working at Pike Place Fish since 2005. He explains, to your dismay, that the fish throwing is actually the easy part. "I agree that what we do is entertaining," he says. "But what we specialize in isn't entertainment." By offering a unique experience to each person that passes by, Pike Place Fish specializes in relationships. And although launching finned friends fifteen feet across huge displays of whole halibut—the shtick that creates those relationships—and flying seafood around the world has brought the company profits and popularity, its newest initiative is driven by a more global goal.

The fun started a quarter century ago, when the folks at Pike Place Fish were looking for clever ways to catch more business without much of a marketing budget. They realized that, while they were known as a place to procure great seafood, they didn't have the kind of customer relationships that made each interaction so memorable that people felt compelled to keep talking about it. So they set about coming up with a game that would facilitate an interaction with every person that passed their stand, whether or not they were there to buy fish. The implied goal—just a joke, at first—was to become world famous. Slowly and organically, throwing fish over the counter from the displays in the front, a habit they used for efficiency when they were too busy with customers to walk the fish up to the registers, became just that game.

The game evolved: each time a customer requested, say, a halibut fillet, an employee shouted "HALIBUT!" to announce the purchase. Eight other voices immediately echoed "HALIBUT!" and someone threw the fish over the counter to be packaged. The ploy worked; visitors laughed and smiled, and ultimately walked away not only with fish, but also with an experience worth repeating. It was social networking before there was social networking.

The lasting advantage, says Taho, wasn't just selling more fish: Pike Place Fish has thrived because the team environment the game created made it a stable, cohesive company that treats every customer interaction—regardless of whether a sale is involved—as an emotional event. The management saw service and efficiency improve as the fishmongers began to value the context in which they worked. The theatrics encouraged people to ask questions about the fish, and people like Taho started doubling as educators, talking face-to-face with visitors about the products' origins and what to do with them in the kitchen.

The events of September 11, 2001, caused Pike Place Fish's owners to rethink their goal. Being world famous is one thing, but given its ability to connect with a huge percentage of the roughly ten million tourists that come through the Market each year, Pike Place Fish started formulating a new, broader goal—after achieving world fame, it set out to do its part toward world peace.

It sounds trite, of course. But since the business offered the opportunity to educate literally millions of people each year on some of the issues surrounding environmental change—an undeniable component to world peace, according to Taho—Pike Place Fish launched a sustainability initiative. It partnered with the Monterey Bay Aquarium and the Marine Stewardship Council to reevaluate the seafood industry, changing suppliers when necessary and stocking its cases differently with the new goal of selling only sustainably harvested seafood. In early 2011, after a brief closure for remodeling, Pike Place Fish reopened, selling only sustainably caught fish and shellfish.

Because many of Pike Place Fish's products come from Alaska, where fisheries have been for the most part sustainable since before it was a mainstream issue, some of its sources have stayed the same. But the purveyor no longer sells things like net-caught yellowfin tuna, trawled scallops, monkfish, or foreign shrimp, all of which have significant bycatch issues. And some prices have gone up—which, according to Taho, is exactly what needs to happen, if the objective is to raise awareness about the environmental issues surrounding fish.

"When people ask why our prices have risen, we have the opportunity to educate them about sustainability," says Taho. "Whether or not they buy fish is not the point. The point is that they get to decide how to spend their money, which is one of the most powerful political decisions a person can make. People walk away knowing more."

Much like when Pike Place Fish made the switch to throwing and catching its fish, the sustainability initiative has changed the company on the inside too. Fishmongers now know more about various fishes' life cycles and habitats, and about the policies that dictate catch guidelines, which have a big effect on pricing. New composting and recycling practices behind the counter take a bit more mental energy, which Taho says makes every employee more cognizant of the little details that make a fish market run smoothly, from filling the displays with ice to using the most efficient lighting.

"Do people walk away without fish when they see the price of wild-caught king salmon in the winter? Sure," says Taho. But because of the flying fish, Pike Place Fish did succeed in catching their attention in the first place. And every good fisherman knows that, sometimes, there's more sport in catch and release.

NORTHWEST EGGS BENEDICT

recipe by **Kerry Sear, of ART Restaurant & Lounge**

If there were a luxurious start to a Pike Place Market tour, it would begin just south of the Market at ART, the restaurant in the Four Seasons Hotel, with smoked salmon Benedict. Swathed in velvety hollandaise sauce, chef Kerry Sear's version pairs best with a view of Puget Sound, great coffee, and a glass of fresh-squeezed juice. ART has them all.

This recipe allows for one egg per person; double it for bigger portions. Also, this is a relatively light hollandaise–add a squeeze of lemon if you like it tangy.

active time **45 minutes** │ *makes* **6 servings**

½ cup dry white wine
1 small shallot, finely chopped
1 sprig fresh tarragon, plus 2 tablespoons chopped fresh tarragon for garnish
4 large egg yolks
1 cup (2 sticks) unsalted butter, cut into tablespoons, at room temperature
Kosher salt and freshly ground white pepper
1 tablespoon white vinegar
6 large eggs
3 english muffins, split, toasted, and buttered
12 slices smoked salmon

■ Start by making the hollandaise: In a small saucepan, simmer the wine, shallot, and tarragon sprig until the liquid has been reduced by about half. Strain the mixture into the top portion of a double boiler, discarding the solids. Whisk the egg yolks into the liquid, then set the double boiler over low heat. Whisking continuously, add the butter one tablespoon at a time, adding more only when the heat of the eggs has melted the previous piece entirely. Season the sauce to taste with salt and pepper and set aside off the heat (but still sitting over the hot water); this is your hollandaise. Stir occasionally to keep warm.

■ Just before serving, poach the eggs: Fill a large, wide saucepan or high-sided skillet with about 2 inches of water and bring to a bare simmer. Add the vinegar (this helps keep the eggs together as they poach). Crack each egg into a ramekin or small bowl. Carefully lower the eggs into the simmering water, tipping them out of their ramekins right at the water's surface, and poach for 4 to 6 minutes, depending on how you like your yolks. (If you don't have a pan at least 12 inches in diameter, use two pans and 1 tablespoon vinegar for each.)

■ Top each english muffin half with 2 slices of smoked salmon. When the eggs are done, carefully remove them with a slotted spoon and blot gently with paper towels. Set one egg on each muffin, on top of the salmon, drizzle with hollandaise, and garnish with the chopped tarragon. Serve immediately.

ETTA'S MINI DUNGENESS CRAB CAKES
with GREEN COCKTAIL SAUCE

recipe by **Tom Douglas, of Etta's**

At the end of many Savor Seattle Food Tours, the laugh-a-minute trips through the Pike Place Market that woo visitors with tastes of Market specialties, you'll get a bite of Etta's famous crab cakes–perfect timing if you're of the save-the-best-for-last mind-set. These mini versions are perfect as handheld appetizers.

Panko is a Japanese style of bread crumbs that are coarser than regular bread crumbs and stay nice and crisp when fried. Look for panko in Japanese and other Asian markets, fish markets, and many large supermarkets.

active time **40 minutes** | *makes* **about 12 small crab cakes**

½ pound Dungeness crabmeat, drained, picked clean of shells, and squeezed of any excess liquid
⅔ cup mayonnaise or Homemade Aioli (page 184)
1 tablespoon plus 1 teaspoon grated lemon zest (about 2 small lemons)
1 tablespoon plus 1 teaspoon finely snipped fresh dill
1 tablespoon plus 1 teaspoon finely snipxped fresh chives
Kosher salt and freshly ground black pepper
¼ cup panko plus ¾ cup for dredging
2 tablespoons unsalted butter
1 cup Green Cocktail Sauce (recipe follows)

- In a large bowl with a rubber spatula, gently combine the crabmeat, mayonnaise, lemon zest, dill, chives, and salt and pepper to taste. Add ¼ cup of the panko and mix again. Put the remaining panko in a shallow bowl.

- Form the crab mixture into 12 golf ball–size mounds. Gently pat them into ½-inch-thick disks without squishing them. Drop the cakes into the panko and turn them to coat both sides, patting to shake off the excess. Let the crab cakes chill in the refrigerator for at least one hour, or up to 24 hours, before frying.

- Preheat the oven to 450°F.

- Heat a large nonstick ovenproof skillet (or two smaller skillets) over medium-high heat and add the butter. When the butter is melted, turn the pan to distribute it evenly, and add the crab cakes. Leave the pan on the burner for about a minute (the butter should not brown), then transfer the pan to the oven. Cook the crab cakes until they are heated through and golden brown on both sides, about 10 minutes, carefully turning them with a spatula about halfway through the baking time. (If you want the best crust, turn your crab cakes once while they're in the oven, but don't disturb them any more than that.) Transfer the crab cakes to plates and serve immediately, with the green cocktail sauce in a separate bowl, for spooning on top of the cakes.

GREEN COCKTAIL SAUCE

makes **1 cup sauce**

½ pound tomatillos, husked and
 quartered
2 tablespoons rice wine vinegar
1 tablespoon sugar
2 teaspoons green Tabasco sauce
1 teaspoon finely chopped garlic
1 teaspoon mustard seeds, toasted
 (see Market Tip)
1 teaspoon peeled, grated fresh
 horseradish

- Whirl the tomatillos in a food processor or blender until coarsely
 pureed. Transfer the puree to a sieve and drain and discard the liquid.
 Put the puree in a bowl and stir in the vinegar, sugar, green Tabasco,
 garlic, mustard seeds, and horseradish. Serve with the crab cakes.

MARKET TIP: *Toasting Spices*

To toast spices, place them in a small, heavy skillet over medium heat for a few minutes,
shaking or stirring constantly, just until they are lightly browned and aromatic.

SEATOWN PICKLED KING SALMON
with HORSERADISH CREAM

recipe by **Tom Douglas, of Seatown Seabar & Rotisserie**

Seatown, one of the Market area's newest additions (just north of the Market's boundaries), is known for two things: irresistibly fresh seafood and expertly roasted meats. This pickled salmon, served on rye toasts with a sauce of crème fraîche, herbs, and grated fresh horseradish, is similar to pickled herring, but with a firmer texture and a richer flavor. Serve it as an appetizer or part of a brunch.

For the best flavor, buy your spices fresh each time you make this. Also, note that the salmon requires a few days to make, so plan accordingly.

active time **40 minutes** | *makes* **8 servings**

for the **salmon**

4 cups room-temperature water

2 cups kosher salt

1 (3- to 4-pound) side king salmon, deboned, skinned, and cut into ¾-inch pieces

6 cups (two 24-ounce bottles) rice wine vinegar

1 cup mirin (sweet Japanese rice wine)

1½ cups (packed) light brown sugar

1 cup sugar

1 star anise

2 tablespoons whole coriander seeds

1 tablespoon white peppercorns

1 tablespoon mustard seeds

1 teaspoon fennel seeds

1 large onion, thinly sliced

continued

- First, brine the salmon: In a large bowl, stir the water and salt together to blend. Add the salmon chunks, stir to combine, and let sit for 8 to 12 hours, covered and refrigerated.

- Combine the rice wine vinegar, mirin, brown sugar, sugar, star anise, coriander seeds, peppercorns, mustard seeds, fennel seeds, and onion in a large nonreactive soup pot and bring to a simmer. Reduce heat to low and simmer for 20 minutes, stirring occasionally. Set aside to cool to room temperature.

- While the pickling liquid cools, remove the salmon from its brine, discard the brine, and rinse the salmon gently but thoroughly under cold running water. Place the salmon on a cooling rack set over a sheet pan and air dry in the refrigerator, uncovered, for at least 2 hours.

- Add the salmon to the pickling liquid (or combine the ingredients in another container), cover, and let sit, refrigerated, for at least 2 days, and up to 2 weeks.

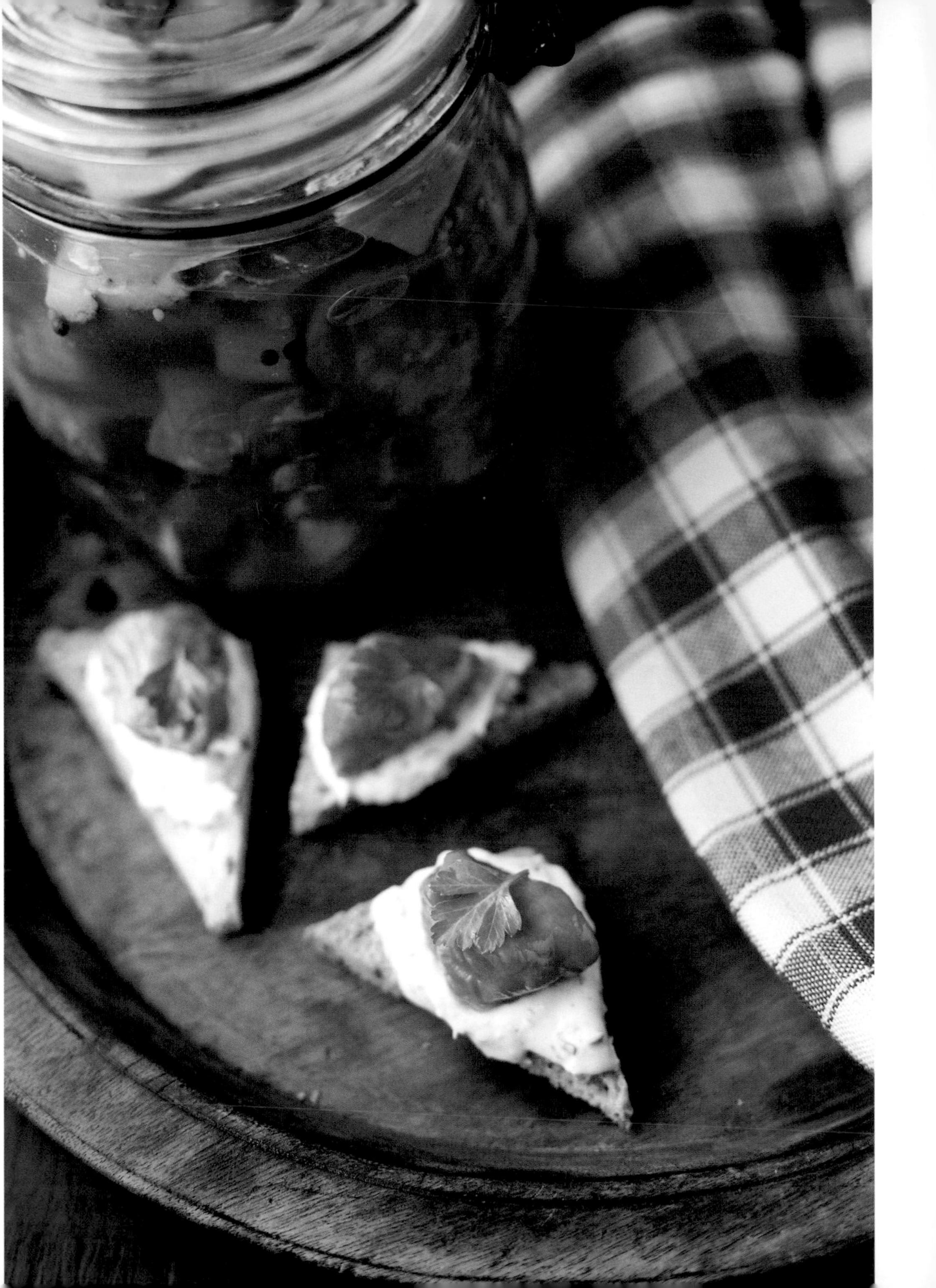

for the horseradish cream

1 cup crème fraîche
2 tablespoons snipped fresh chives
¼ cup finely chopped fresh parsley
2 tablespoons peeled and grated fresh
   horseradish
Kosher salt and freshly ground black
   pepper

Rye toasts, for serving

- Before serving, make the horseradish cream: Stir the crème fraîche, chives, parsley, and horseradish together in a small bowl and season to taste with salt and pepper.

- To serve the salmon, skim off any oil that has accumulated on the surface and strain the fish. Smear horseradish cream on rye toasts and top with salmon.

PIKE PLACE CHOWDER'S MARKET CHOWDER

recipe by **Larry Mellum, of Pike Place Chowder**

Pike Place Chowder is hidden in Post Alley for a good reason: when you're scooping its award-winning New England–style chowder out of a sourdough boule, you really can't handle looking at anything but the other side of a brick-lined alley. It's that good. Although owner Larry Mellum prides himself on using the best Market-fresh ingredients, twenty years of chowder making has taught him that a crucial step is simply keeping it at the right temperature, to avoid overcooking the shellfish. Pike Place Chowder serves it at precisely 155°F. (No one will know if you don't use you thermometer here; the gist of the secret is that it's important not to let the chowder boil.)

This version, which leans on chorizo from Uli's Famous Sausage for spice and fresh-picked crab and chopped oysters for meatiness, is delicious served with sourdough bread or Outrageous Garlic Breadsticks (page 183), for mopping up the last juices.

active time **45 minutes** | *makes* **6 servings**

1 medium (about ¼ pound) red-skinned potato, peeled and quartered

7 tablespoons unsalted butter, divided

1 large link (about ¼ pound) beef or pork chorizo, casing removed, crumbled

½ medium onion, cut into ⅜-inch pieces

3 ribs celery, cut into ⅜-inch pieces

2½ teaspoons Old Bay Seasoning

½ ripe tomato, cut into ⅜-inch pieces

Kernels from 1 ear corn (see page 78 for an easy corn-cutting technique)

½ pound fresh-picked crabmeat

1 quart heavy cream

1 (10-ounce) jar freshly shucked oysters (from about 1 dozen medium oysters), with juice

¼ cup plus 1 tablespoon all-purpose flour

- Place the potato quarters in a small saucepan and add cold water to cover. Bring to a boil over high heat, then reduce to a simmer and cook until the potato is just tender, about 10 to 15 minutes. Drain, chop the potato into ½-inch pieces, and set aside. Reserve the saucepan for later.

- While the potatoes cook, melt 2 tablespoons of the butter in a large, heavy soup pot over medium heat. When it has melted, crumble the chorizo into the pan and cook, undisturbed, for 5 minutes. Add the onion and celery and sauté with a wooden spoon, breaking the chorizo up into small pieces, until the onion is translucent, another 8 to 10 minutes. Add the Old Bay and sauté for about a minute. Add the chopped potatoes, tomato, corn, crabmeat, and cream. Chop and add the oysters, stir well, and heat the mixture, stirring frequently, to 160°F, or until you just begin to see a bit of foam bubbling toward the surface of the soup.

1 (15-ounce) can fish stock, at room temperature
½ cup finely chopped fresh parsley
Kosher salt and freshly ground black pepper

- While the chowder heats, melt the remaining 5 tablespoons of butter over low heat in the same pan you used to cook the potatoes. When melted, add the flour, and cook, stirring constantly, for about a minute. Add the fish stock a little at a time, whisking vigorously to combine between each addition as the mixture thickens. Once you have a smooth sauce, whisk it into the chowder.

- Bring the chowder to 190°F—if you don't have a thermometer, you'll hear the chowder beginning to bubble at the bottom, but you shouldn't bring it all the way to a simmer. Stir in the chopped parsley and hold the chowder at roughly 190°F for 30 minutes, stirring occasionally. (If your stove doesn't have a super-low setting, try alternating between low and off to avoid letting the chowder simmer.) Let the chowder cool to 155°F, season to taste with salt and pepper, and serve hot.

CORNMEAL-CRUSTED PAN-FRIED RAZOR CLAMS *with* MAMA LIL'S DIPPING SAUCE

Razor clams are similar to regular clams in name only; they're a great way to convince someone afraid of shellfish that bivalves are one of nature's finest gifts. Encased in long, thin shells—hence the name—razor clams are a forager's dream. But if you can't get out to Washington's southwestern coast for a clam dig, head to Pike Place Fish, where they're sometimes available whole. (You can almost always buy them frozen.) Ask your fishmonger how to open them, or better yet, have him or her do it for you. Once they're home (and thawed completely, if you're using frozen clams), blot them dry on paper towels, and arrange each clam flat on a cutting board. Using a small, sharp knife, cut out the stomach—the part that's dark inside—so what's left to cook is pure muscle. The clam's digger is thicker than the rest of the clam, but it's the best part to eat. There you have it: a clam with no guts and no sand. Perfect novice clam-eating material.

Regular yellow cornmeal works best for this recipe. If you can't find Mama Lil's pickled peppers, a Seattle specialty available at DeLaurenti, substitute hot Peppadews or another pickled pepper.

active time **35 minutes** | *makes* **4 servings**

for the sauce

1 cup mayonnaise or Homemade Aioli (page 184)
¼ cup finely chopped shallots
¼ cup Mama Lil's peppers (with oil), finely chopped
Juice of ½ medium lemon (about 1½ tablespoons)

for the razor clams

1 pound razor clams, trimmed per headnote directions
Kosher salt and freshly ground black pepper
¼ cup (½ stick) unsalted butter, divided
1 cup cornmeal

- First, make the sauce: In a medium bowl, thoroughly mix the mayonnaise, shallots, peppers, and lemon juice. Set aside.

- Season the razor clams with salt and pepper to taste. Melt 2 tablespoons of the butter in a large skillet over medium-high heat. When the butter has melted, dredge a few of the razor clams in the cornmeal, and cook for about 1 minute per side, or until the clams are golden brown and have curled up a bit, similar to how bacon looks as it cooks. Transfer the clams to a paper towel-lined plate and repeat with the remaining ingredients, adding more butter as necessary. Serve the clams immediately, right as they are removed from the pan, with the sauce for dipping.

BLACKENED SALMON SANDWICHES

Belly up to the lunch counter at Market Grill, in the Pike Place Market's Main Arcade, and you'll be treated to the ultimate grilled fish sandwich. Ask for blackened salmon with rosemary mayo–there aren't many choices, but this one's my favorite–and you'll get a freshly grilled Le Panier baguette piled with grilled onions, romaine, tomatoes, and coho salmon seasoned with MarketSpice's Blackened Redfish Rub. Of course, you'll also need to share a cup of chowder with a friend and top your meal off with the Grill's crunchy, peppery coleslaw.

If you can, buy the salmon and baguette for this recipe at the same time, so you can estimate how much fish it will take to fill each sandwich.

active time **40 minutes** | *makes* **4 sandwiches**

4 roughly 5-by-2-inch skinned coho (or similar) salmon fillets, about ¾-inch thick (2 pounds total)

⅓ cup canola oil, for brushing

1 tablespoon plus 1 teaspoon blackening spice, such as MarketSpice's Blackened Redfish Rub (see Resources, page 193)

1 baguette, cut into 4 equal sections, each halved lengthwise

1 large onion, cut into ½-inch rings

½ cup mayonnaise or Homemade Aioli (page 184)

2 teaspoons chopped fresh rosemary

2 teaspoons freshly squeezed lemon juice

Kosher salt and freshly ground black pepper

8 leaves romaine lettuce

2 tomatoes, sliced

- Prepare a grill for cooking over direct high heat, about 450°F to 500°F.

- Brush the salmon fillets generously on both sides with oil and transfer to a platter. Season each piece with about a teaspoon of the spice (½ teaspoon per side) and set them aside.

- Brush the cut sides of the baguettes and both sides of the onion rings with the oil, and set aside.

- In a small bowl, blend the mayonnaise with the rosemary, lemon juice, and salt and pepper to taste. Set aside.

- When the grill is hot, brush the cooking grates clean, then grill the salmon and onions for about 5 minutes, covered, or until the fish releases easily from the grates. Turn the fish and the onions, and add the baguettes to the sides of the grill, over indirect heat, oiled sides down. Grill another 2 to 3 minutes, or until the salmon is cooked through, the onions are soft, and the bread is toasted.

- Arrange 2 romaine leaves on each bottom baguette piece. Top each with tomatoes, then a piece of grilled fish, then a pile of grilled onions. Slather the top baguette pieces with the mayonnaise, cap the sandwiches, and serve immediately.

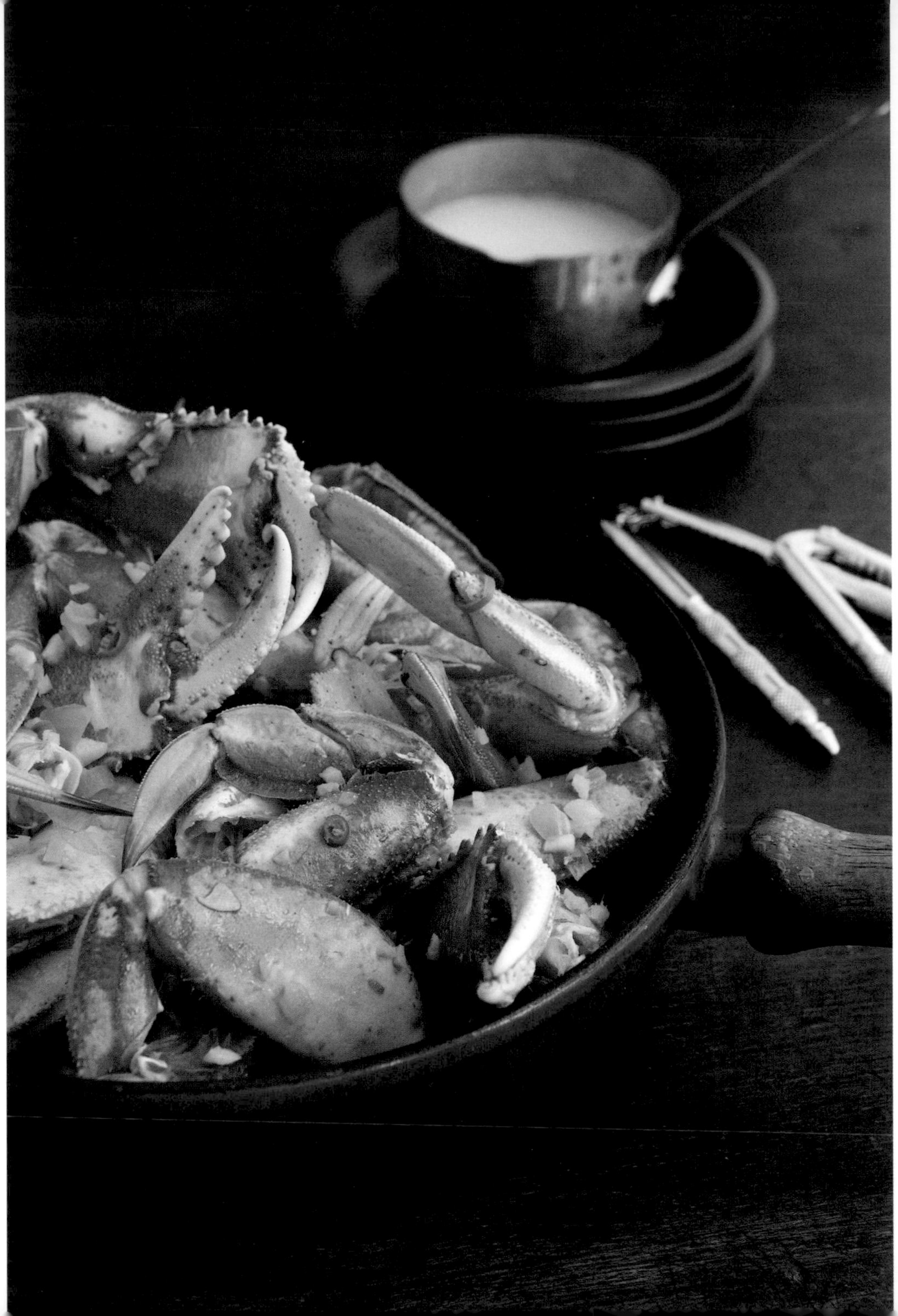

SAUTÉED CRAB LEGS *with* CHILI-GINGER BUTTER

If the only thing that stands between you and your regular crab dinner is the thought of smelling cooked crab in your bedroom the morning after, hit Pure Food Fish in the Market's Main Arcade. From your safe spot in front of the cooked crab display, you can pick which creatures you want to take home, and someone will prep them for you—so while you traipse home with the crab legs for this spicy, gingery crab feast, someone with a much fishier trash handles the bodies.

Not one bit of flavor is wasted, as the shallots, ginger, and Thai chilies used to cook the shellfish do double duty in the butter, served in little bowls alongside everyone's plate. This tasty sauce is meant for dipping, but it's so good, if you insist on drinking it, I won't judge you.

For four people, serve the crab with two baguettes (no one will want to leave any juices behind) and a big salad, such as the Warm Panzanella Salad with Blistered Tomatoes, Corn, and Basil (page 139).

active time **25 minutes** | *makes* **4 servings**

1 tablespoon olive oil
1 large shallot, finely chopped
2 or 3 Thai chilies (to taste), very thinly sliced
2 large cloves garlic, minced
2 tablespoons peeled, finely chopped fresh ginger (from a thumb-size piece)
½ cup dry white wine
1 (8-ounce) bottle clam juice
3 pounds cooked crab legs, from 3 cooked Dungeness crabs (see Market Tip)
½ cup (1 stick) unsalted butter, cut into chunks, at room temperature

- Heat the oil in a large, wide soup pot over medium heat until it shimmers. Add the shallot and cook, stirring occasionally, for 3 minutes, or until soft. Add the chilies, garlic, and ginger, and cook, stirring continuously, for about a minute. Add the wine and clam juice, bring to a strong simmer, and cook for 2 minutes. Add the crab legs, cover tightly, and cook for about 5 minutes, or until the crab is heated through, stirring the legs around once to coat them in the ginger and chilies.

- Using tongs, pile the hot crab into a serving bowl. Add the butter to the pot, and whisk until just melted. Divide the chili-ginger butter among four small bowls and serve immediately, with the hot crab.

MARKET TIP: *Buying Crab Legs*

Crabs are fragile and sometimes their legs fall off in transport. Ask your fishmonger if he or she has single legs for sale; it's often less expensive than buying whole crabs and taking the legs off yourself.

CLAM, MUSSEL, *and* WHITE BEAN PAELLA

recipe by **Steve Winston, of The Spanish Table**

At The Spanish Table, where owner Steve Winston has been selling all things Iberian since 1995, only the types of beans available upstage his selection of paella pans. In this atypical (and unusually simple) paella, he combines *granja* beans with manila clams, mussels from the Pacific Northwest, and sole. As the Spanish *bomba* rice cooks and forms a thin, crisp crust at the bottom of the paella pan, the beans become sweet and creamy.

Winston says that paella is distinguished from Italy's risotto in that it is cooked using olive oil rather than butter, cheese, or cream and the Valencian rice (such as *bomba*) grains remain distinct (rather than creaming together) because they don't have as much surface starch. For this reason, once assembled, paella is never stirred. The cook's job is to stand back and wait, with a glass of wine in hand.

Serve with fresh Market greens dressed with sherry vinegar, Spanish olive oil, and crumbled Cabrales (Spanish blue) cheese.

For instructions on cooking beans, see page 77. Look for *granja* and *bomba* at The Spanish Table.

active time **1 hour** | *makes* **6 servings** | *special equipment* **1 (14-inch) paella pan**

2 pounds manila clams
1 pound mussels
¼ cup Spanish olive oil
2 cloves garlic, finely chopped
1 pound Dover sole or other mild white fish, cut into 1-inch pieces
Pinch of Spanish saffron
4 cups (four 8-ounce bottles) clam juice
2 cups *bomba* (Valencian short-grain rice)
1 cup *granja* or other large white beans, cooked al dente

- First, rinse the clams and mussels, and place them in a bowl of cold water. Set aside for 15 minutes; the shellfish will siphon out any extra sand and grit.

- Heat the olive oil and garlic over medium heat in a 12- or 14-inch paella pan or a large cast-iron skillet. When the garlic starts to sizzle, add the sole and cook for 1 to 2 minutes on each side, or until the fish turns white. Sprinkle the saffron over the fish, then add the clam juice and bring to a strong simmer. Stir in the rice and the cooked beans, and return to a simmer. Drain and rinse the shellfish and remove any byssus threads, also known as "beards," from the mussels (these little hairy parts connect the mussels to their environment while they're alive). Arrange the clams and mussels right on top of the rice and beans, hinged sides down.

- Simmer the paella on medium-low heat for about 30 to 45 minutes, or until the rice is cooked and all the shellfish have opened. (Discard any that do not open.) The clams and mussels will probably release enough liquid that the pan will not go dry before the rice is cooked, but if they don't, add a little water–not too much, or you won't get the *socarrat*, the crust of rice that forms on the bottom of the pan just as the paella is done. (Listen carefully, and you can hear the rice crackle and pop as it forms.)

- Serve hot. (Tradition dictates that paella be lightly covered for 10 minutes after it is cooked, before serving, but your guests might not be that patient.)

NOTE: It's best to use your biggest burner for this recipe, to ensure heat under the entire paella pan. If your paella only seems to be cooking in the middle, rotate the pan every few minutes, so the flame is under a different part each time, or transfer the paella to a 350°F oven after about 20 minutes and let it finish cooking there.

MARKET TIP: *Debearding Mussels*

Although many farmed mussels don't develop large "beards," the small bunch of threads that connect them to where they're growing, most wild ones do. To prepare wild mussels (and spiff up farmed species), first wash them well, then discard any that are broken or that don't close when you gently squeeze the shells. Immediately before cooking, debeard them: Use your thumb and first finger to grasp the beard, and pull it out by yanking perpendicular toward the mussel hinge.

GRILLED OCTOPUS *and* CHICKPEA SALAD

recipe by **Mike Easton, of Lecosho**

Among the myriad options offered by the Pike Place Market's fishmongers, you may find a spotted, curly, purple arm. It belongs to an octopus. And although they may be scary to look at, they're actually quite simple to cook, as long as you follow one simple rule: They must be cooked until tender. At Lecosho, the restaurant Matt Janke opened after leaving Matt's in the Market, they grill tender octopus and mix it with chickpeas and a spicy vinaigrette made with Seattle-based Mama Lil's peppers, for a unique and satisfying warm salad. Serve it tapas-style on small plates or make it a meal by heaping it on fresh greens.

You'll need to begin the day before if you're starting with dried chickpeas, but you can substitute three 15-ounce cans of chickpeas if you'd like and simmer them with the other chickpea ingredients for 20 minutes before folding them into the salad.

Note that octopuses weigh much more than you might expect—although this recipe calls for nine pounds, you're not really going to eat nine pounds of octopus; much of it is water weight that cooks out. If you can't find octopus, substitute a pound of medium shrimp, and grill them before adding them to the salad. City Fish usually carries frozen octopus; call a day ahead and ask them to thaw it for you.

active time **45 minutes** | *makes* **4 to 6 servings**

for the **chickpeas**

1 pound dried chickpeas
1 onion, diced
1 carrot, peeled and diced
1 rib celery, diced
3 bay leaves
1 sprig fresh thyme
2 tablespoons kosher salt

for the **octopus**

3 (3-pound) whole octopuses, fresh
   or frozen
6 bay leaves
7 whole cloves
1 teaspoon red pepper flakes
1 teaspoon whole fennel seeds
2 tablespoons kosher salt

- The night before serving, start the chickpeas: Place the chickpeas in a large soup pot and add cold water to cover by at least 3 inches. Set aside to soak overnight.

- The next day, cook the octopus and chickpeas: Place the whole octopuses, along with the bay leaves, cloves, red pepper flakes, fennel seeds, and salt, in a large pot and add cold water to cover. Bring to a simmer and cook, partially covered, turning the octopuses occasionally, until they are bright purple, curly, and completely tender when poked through with a skewer, about 2 to 3 hours (depending on the size). Transfer the octopuses to a plate, slice off the tentacles at their base, and cut the tentacles into bite-size pieces.

for the vinaigrette

1 cup pickled hot peppers in oil (such as Mama Lil's), measured with oil, plus ¼ cup oil from the jar
1 clove garlic, crushed
1 small shallot, roughly chopped
1 tablespoon Dijon mustard
1 tablespoon honey
Pinch of cayenne (optional)
¼ cup sherry vinegar
¼ cup extra-virgin olive oil
Kosher salt and freshly ground black pepper
¼ cup roughly chopped fresh parsley

■ While the octopuses cook, drain the chickpeas. In the pot you used to soak them, add the onion, carrot, celery, bay leaves, and thyme, and add water to cover by about 4 inches. Bring the mixture to a boil, then turn the heat down and simmer until tender, about 1 hour. When the chickpeas are tender, stir in the salt and let sit for 10 minutes. Drain the chickpeas, transfer them to a large mixing bowl, and remove the bay leaves and thyme stem.

■ While the chickpeas cook, make the vinaigrette: In a blender or food processor, whirl the peppers (but not the extra ¼ cup oil), garlic, shallot, mustard, honey, cayenne, and sherry vinegar until uniform. With the machine on, add the olive oil and the reserved oil from the peppers to the vinaigrette in a slow, steady stream. Season to taste with salt and pepper, then pour the dressing over the warm chickpeas. Add the parsley and the chopped octopus, stir to blend, and serve warm or at room temperature.

NOTE: If you'd like to cook the octopuses ahead of time, do what the chef does: let them cool to room temperature in their cooking brine, then refrigerate for up to 24 hours. Before serving, drain them and sear on a hot grill for a minute or two before adding to the salad.

SEARED SALMON *with* TWO-CHERRY RELISH

There is perhaps nothing more emblematic of the Pike Place Market than a fillet of salmon—unless it's a fillet of salmon topped with a shallot- and chive-studded cherry relish, made with a mix of blushing golden Rainier and brick-red bing varieties. This is Market cooking at its simplest. At the peak of cherry season, serve this with grilled zucchini or asparagus, a simple salad, and crusty bread.

active time **25 minutes** | *makes* **6 servings**

1 small shallot, finely chopped
½ pound bing cherries, halved and pitted
½ pound Rainier cherries, halved and pitted
1 tablespoon sherry vinegar
2 tablespoons snipped fresh chives
Kosher salt and freshly ground black pepper
6 (1-inch-thick) salmon fillets (about 2½ pounds total), skin left on
1 tablespoon olive oil

- First, make the relish: In a medium mixing bowl, combine the shallot, bings, Rainiers, vinegar, chives, and salt and pepper to taste. Set aside.

- Heat two large, heavy skillets over medium heat. (If you don't have two skillets, cook the salmon in two batches.) While the pans heat, brush the salmon generously with the olive oil, then season to taste with salt and pepper.

- When the pans are hot, add the salmon fillets, skin side up, and cook for about 10 minutes, turning the fish roughly halfway through only when it releases easily from the pan. When the fillets are firm in the center and just beginning to release white fat (albumin) from the edges, slide a spatula between the fish and the skin of each piece and transfer the fish to a serving platter, leaving the skin behind. Heap the relish on top and serve immediately.

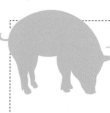

MARKET TIP: *Buying and Cooking Salmon*

When buying salmon, look for firm flesh, shiny scales that aren't sloughing off, and clear (as opposed to cloudy) eyes. When you cook it, you'll know it's done when you just begin to see the beginnings of small beads of fat escaping at the edges—the flesh should still be a bit shiny in the center.

RIGATONI *with* SMOKED SALMON, KALE, *and* GOAT CHEESE

Traditionally slow smoked over an alderwood fire, Totem Smokehouse's salmon has a dry, flaky texture that allows it to blend into the cream sauce for this relatively quick pasta dish. Choose a basic smoked salmon, like Totem's smoked sockeye, or something with a bit of a kick, like its spicier varieties–just don't use the cured, presliced kind you associate with bagels. Before you start, taste your salmon. If it seems salty, skip the salt in the recipe.

active time **20 minutes** | *makes* **2 large or 4 small servings**

3 cups (about 10 ounces) rigatoni, or other bite-size pasta

1 tablespoon olive oil

½ bunch (about ¼ pound) lacinato kale, finely chopped (about 2 cups)

Kosher salt and freshly ground black pepper

½ cup heavy cream

1 cup skinned and roughly chopped smoked salmon (from 8 ounces smoked salmon)

4 ounces goat cheese, crumbled

- Put a pot of salted water on for the pasta. When the water boils, cook the rigatoni al dente according to package instructions.

- While the pasta cooks, heat the oil over medium heat in a large sauté pan. Add the kale and cook, stirring, until it is wilted, 5 minutes or so. Season to taste with salt and pepper, add the cream and salmon, stir, and simmer on the lowest heat until the pasta is done, 2 to 3 minutes more.

- Drain the pasta, reserving about ½ cup pasta water. Add the pasta to the salmon/kale mixture, along with a bit of the water (more if you'd like a looser sauce) and about three-quarters of the goat cheese, and stir over low heat until the mixture is warmed through and the cheese is melted. Serve hot, sprinkled with pepper and the remaining goat cheese.

WILD WATERS: *Not All Salmon Tastes the Same*

Saying you're having salmon for dinner is a little like saying you like the taste of vegetables; it's accurate, but not exactly descriptive, because like vegetables, different species of salmon have vastly different tastes. With varying degrees of fattiness, individual diets, and unique environments, one salmon species can have a richer flavor, while others taste quite lean. The texture of the flesh also varies depending on how the fish is treated after the catch. Some species, like pink and keta, are best caught in salt water, because their meat loses firmness as they return to freshwater to spawn. (This is why they're used most often for canning and smoking, respectively, even though they're both delicious fresh.)

Here's a rundown of the most popular wild Pacific species, listed from largest to smallest. Note that, in addition to this, salmon are also often sold by their place of origin: Copper River salmon, for example, are from Alaska.

KING (or chinook) salmon are the biggest species, sometimes weighing up to 125 pounds. With a pretty, iridescent sheen on their tails, kings are prized for their rich, fatty flesh—and they're usually the most expensive.

KETA (or chum) salmon have the mildest flavor and drier flesh than other species, making them suitable for smoking and a great base for flavorful wet rubs. Keta are also called dog salmon, because the males grow big canine-like teeth as they get close to freshwater.

COHO (or silver) salmon are often identified by the little black spots along their back. They have slightly orange-colored flesh and are oily but not overpowering, as some people find sockeye.

SOCKEYE salmon, which are also called bluebacks because they can have a blue tint to them, have the strongest salmon flavor, with very red flesh. The meat is quite firm.

PINK salmon are usually the smallest and have the most remarkable hump on their back as they enter freshwater. They also have a shorter life cycle than other salmon. Pink fillets are thinner and more delicate, and should be cooked for less time. Most canned salmon is pink salmon because in large commercial operations, it's difficult not to bruise the fishes' flesh during catching and handling.

STEELHEAD salmon, with their colorful, spotted backs, live up to four years in freshwater before migrating out to sea—and some don't ever leave, in which case they're called steelhead trout.

10 WAYS 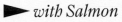 ► *with Salmon*

QUICK SALMON RILLETTES
Blend ½ pound cooked salmon with 1 stick softened unsalted butter, salt and pepper to taste, and 1 tablespoon snipped fresh chives. Spread on baguette slices and sprinkle with goat cheese and extra chives before serving.

GRILLED COCONUT-GINGER SALMON
In a large bowl, stir together 1 can regular coconut milk, the zest and juice of a large lime, 2 tablespoons grated peeled fresh ginger, ½ cup finely chopped cilantro, and a squeeze of *sriracha* (spicy chile) sauce to taste. Marinate 4 (6-ounce) salmon fillets for 30 minutes. Grill over high heat, flesh side down first.

SALMON TACOS *with* HOT-SWEET MANGO SLAW
Make Hot-Sweet Mango Pickles (page 99), only instead of slicing the mango, grate it in a food processor. Pile grilled salmon, thinly sliced avocado, shredded red cabbage, and the mango slaw into small corn tortillas.

SMOKED SALMON-CUCUMBER CANAPÉS
Drape thin slices of salmon lox on thick English cucumber slices. Top with a dollop of crème fraîche and a sprig of dill or chervil, or Garlicky Goat Cheese Mousse (page 87).

KING SALMON *with* OLIVE SALSA
Chop and stir together 1 large clove garlic, minced; 1 tablespoon capers; 1 cup pitted kalamata olives; and ½ cup fresh parsley. Season with olive oil, salt, and pepper to taste, and pack on and around a 2-pound king salmon fillet. Roast at 425°F for 10 to 15 minutes, depending on thickness.

SMOKED SALMON *and* FETA SCRAMBLE
Stir flaked smoked salmon, chopped green onions, and crumbled fresh feta into eggs as you're almost finished scrambling them. (You can also bake the same ingredients into the Spring Frittata

with Morels, Asparagus, Peas, and Ramps on page 36, instead of using the vegetables outlined there.)

QUICKEST BAKED SALMON

For each 1-inch-thick salmon fillet, mix together 1 tablespoon regular cream cheese with 1 tablespoon spicy, chunky salsa. Spread onto the salmon and bake for 8 to 10 minutes at 400°F. (You can also use plain Greek-style yogurt mixed with harissa, described on page 100.)

SALMON CAKES *with* CORN *and* HOT PEPPERS

Pulse 1 pound raw salmon; 1 seeded, chopped jalapeño; 1 seeded, chopped red serrano pepper; 2 cloves garlic; and ½ cup chopped onion in a food processor until well blended. Transfer the mixture to a bowl and stir in 2 large eggs, 2 tablespoons salsa, ½ cup fresh corn (see page 78 for an easy corn-cutting technique), and ½ cup bread crumbs. Season to taste with salt and pepper, and fry golf ball–size portions into cakes in ¼-inch-deep canola oil.

SALMON TOASTS *with* CAPER-DILL CREAM CHEESE

Stir 4 ounces (½ package) regular cream cheese together with 2 tablespoons finely chopped capers, the zest and juice of a small lemon, salt and pepper to taste, and 1 teaspoon dried dill. Spread on crackers and top with smoked salmon flakes.

NORTHWEST NIÇOISE

Make a Northwest version of the French classic: pile a plate with steamed new potatoes and haricots verts, plus chopped tomatoes, quartered hard-cooked eggs, and Niçoise olives. Nestle in a piece of simply cooked salmon and drizzle with Basic French Vinaigrette (page 186).

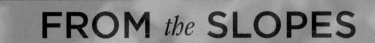

FROM *the* SLOPES

RECIPE LIST

I'D TELL YOU, BUT I'D HAVE TO KILL YOU:

An Urban Mushroom Hunt in the Pike Place Market, with Seattle's Favorite Forager

The most surprising thing Langdon Cook says is that it's OK to wash mushrooms. "I mean, don't bathe them like your child, but run them under cold water to get the dirt and any insect friends off them. They're made to withstand the rain in the forest, so why shouldn't they get wet at home?"

He has a point. And after years of painstakingly swabbing off my mushrooms with a paper towel, I suddenly feel a little less nervous about loading up on the fresh fall varieties Lang is showing me at Sosio's Produce, one of the Pike Place Market's best produce purveyors and its mushroom specialist. A dedicated Seattle-based forager and author of *Fat of the Land*, which chronicles his years foraging for wild edibles in the Pacific Northwest, Lang is celebrated for his intimate knowledge of wild foods, among them the black trumpet, chanterelle, and hedgehog mushrooms displayed before us. Like any forager, Lang keeps his best hunting grounds secret, so it's no use asking him where to find his favorites. "I'd tell you, but I'd have to kill you," he says. Instead, he joined me for an easy late-November hunt—no rain gear required—at the Market, to explain a few different varieties and share tips and tricks for cooking with wild mushrooms.

Fall is high season for chanterelles in Washington, and the season is long, usually spanning from August to November. Soft and buttery yellow, they have smooth, wavy-edged caps that vary in size (exceptionally large mushrooms are often called "flags"). They're gorgeous.

But if chanterelles are the beauty queens of the fall mushroom season, black trumpets are the gangsters. "If you've never seen one before, in the wild, you might think a black trumpet mushroom looks like a thick dead leaf, all curled up from spending a few weeks on the forest floor," says Lang. They do look like rather lifeless little vegetal trumpets, but their flavor is much more exotic, like a very condensed, meaty version of chanterelles. Lang points out that black trumpet mushrooms are one of the few black foods we eat—which is why the French call them the "trumpet of death." In Washington, late in the season, trumpets only grow in one little patch, near the coast.

We move on to hedgehog mushrooms, which are slightly lighter in color than chanterelles—more creamy than buttery—but look similar, until we turn them over. Underneath, Lang shows me how a hedgehog releases its spores from thousands of little quills, instead of the gills (the ribs on the underneath side of the cap) most specimens have. The texture is undeniably hedgehog-like, and the flavor is spicier than a chanterelle's, like they've been sprinkled with cinnamon or cloves.

It's not porcini season, but Lang describes their dual personality—fresh in the spring or fall,

they have a delicate, almost floral flavor. Only after drying do they acquire the deep, earthy flavor they're more typically known for.

And today, there are black truffles. Truffle hunting is a unique art, to say the least. Here in Washington, instead of following the pigs traditionally used in Europe, foragers watch the habits of flying squirrels and voles to figure out where to dig. At Sosio's, Lang picks up a fresh black truffle and smells where it's been sliced—he can tell it's ready to eat because it smells like overripe pineapple.

Our conversation turns to cooking. In the kitchen, Lang thinks of mushrooms as comfort food. Mushrooms aren't afraid of butter or cream—in fact, many of the chemical compounds that make them delicious are fat soluble, which means that combining them with rich ingredients often brings out their flavor.

Two stomachs grumble, so we set out for Lecosho, the restaurant at the far southern end of Post Alley, where we've heard the Wild Mushroom Tagliatelle (see recipe on page 39) can't be missed. Today, the chef's house-made pasta is twirled up with black trumpet mushrooms and an indecent

amount of cream, which we devour, letting the noodles whip up and slap our lips. Lang tells me about how he stores his mushrooms at home—he dries and freezes most varieties or stores them fresh in paper bags in his refrigerator. At this time of year, when his supply of spring morels and porcini is drying up, but his fall mushrooms aren't ready yet, he flavors soups and stews with porcini powder, a dust made from dried, ground mushrooms. I've never used it, but when he describes how it almost magically adds a deep earthiness to his oxtail ragù, I feel like I'm yearning for something illicit.

At DeLaurenti, the specialty store at the corner of First Avenue and Pike Street, Lang shows me small containers of freshly ground porcini powder. At home, I sprinkle it over sautéed onions, garlic, carrots, and celery, and let the deep, dusty scent waft up for a moment before adding the rest of the ingredients to my vegetarian *pasta e fagioli*. In the end, it's the meatiest version I've ever made; my vegetarian friends are skeptical. "What's *in* this?" they ask.

It's hard not to be coy. "I went mushroom foraging," I told them. "So I'd tell you, but I'd have to kill you."

MARKET TIP: *Storing Mushrooms*

Langdon Cook recommends storing fresh mushrooms in a paper bag–never in plastic–in the refrigerator.

BUCKWHEAT PANCAKES
with HUCKLEBERRY SYRUP *and* MASCARPONE

recipe by **Tom Douglas, of Seatown Seabar & Rotisserie**

If you hike in Washington's Cascade Mountains in September, chances are good your knees will brush up against short bushes with deep purple berries bursting from every branch. They're huckleberries–tangier than blueberries, smaller, and sometimes a bit sweeter, they're a local favorite when the season hits. At Tom Douglas's Seatown, across the street from the Pike Place Market, the kitchen whirls them into a syrup and pours it over tender buckwheat pancakes.

This may seem like a lot of batter, but each pancake requires almost a cup of it. Also, unlike most pancake batter, this one is yeast-raised, which means you must allow it time to rise after mixing it. However, it must be used right away–store any leftovers in pancake form.

active time **50 minutes** | *makes* **4 servings**

for the **pancakes**

2⅔ cups whole milk
½ cup (1 stick) unsalted butter, cut into pieces
1⅓ cups all-purpose flour
1⅓ cups buckwheat flour
2 packages (½ ounce, or about 4 teaspoons) active dry yeast
¼ cup sugar
½ teaspoon kosher salt
4 large eggs, lightly beaten

for the **syrup**

2 cups (10 ounces) fresh or frozen huckleberries (see Note)
⅔ cup sugar
1 tablespoon water

3 tablespoons melted butter for cooking pancakes
Mascarpone cheese for serving

- First, combine the milk and butter in a small saucepan. Cook over low heat for a few minutes, only until the milk is warm and the butter is melted (105°F to 115°F).

- Whisk the all-purpose flour, buckwheat flour, yeast, sugar, and salt together in a large bowl, then stir in the milk/butter mixture until combined. Add the eggs and beat by hand until smooth.

- Cover the bowl with plastic wrap and allow the batter to rise in a warm place for 30 to 45 minutes, or until it has doubled in size and is bubbly on the top.

- Meanwhile, make the syrup: Combine the huckleberries, sugar, and water in a small saucepan. Bring to a simmer over medium heat, reduce heat to low, and cook for 10 minutes, stirring occasionally, until most of the berries have burst. Puree the berries in a blender, then transfer to a serving pitcher. Set aside.

- Heat a pancake griddle or large nonstick pan over medium-low heat. Brush with a thin layer of butter and cook the pancakes one at a time. (For large pancakes, use 1 full cup of batter, less for smaller pancakes.) Serve each with a dab of syrup (a little goes a long way) and a spoonful of mascarpone.

NOTE: Blueberries or blackberries are perfectly acceptable substitutes for the huckleberries. If you use blackberries, you may want to strain the seeds out of the syrup before serving.

SPRING FRITTATA *with* MORELS, ASPARAGUS, PEAS, *and* RAMPS

Each spring, Frank's Quality Produce sells ramps, which are early-season members of the allium family that look like green onions with lipstick on, but taste a lot more like garlic. The flavor does wonders for eggs. This frittata, made with other seasonal produce and extra egg whites for lightness, is no exception.

Outside of morel season, you can use quartered or sliced cremini mushrooms instead.

active time **15 minutes** | *makes* **4 to 6 servings**

4 large egg whites
4 large eggs
½ cup whole milk
¼ cup grated Parmesan cheese, divided
4 teaspoons olive oil, divided
¼ pound morel mushrooms, rinsed, trimmed, and halved (quartered if large)
Kosher salt and freshly ground black pepper
10 ramps, chopped (pink and white parts only, about 2 heaping tablespoons chopped)
10 thin asparagus spears, ends trimmed, chopped into 1-inch pieces
⅓ cup English peas or thawed frozen peas

- Preheat the oven to 400°F.

- First, in a medium bowl, whisk the egg whites and eggs until blended and very frothy, about 100 strokes. Whisk in the whole milk and 2 tablespoons of the Parmesan. Set aside.

- Heat a medium ovenproof skillet over medium heat. When hot, add 2 teaspoons of the oil, then the mushrooms, and season to taste with salt and pepper. Cook, stirring occasionally, for 2 to 3 minutes, or until the mushrooms begin to give off their water. Add the remaining 2 teaspoons oil, then the ramps, asparagus, and peas, and cook another minute or so, stirring. Season to taste with salt and pepper. Whisk the egg mixture again, then pour it over the top. Sprinkle the remaining 2 tablespoons of Parmesan over the eggs and vegetables.

- Carefully transfer the frittata to the middle rack of the oven and bake for 20 minutes, or until puffed and golden. Cool for 5 minutes, then slice into wedges and serve hot.

BRIE *with* SAUTÉED CHANTERELLES

In the fall, the hills near Seattle are filled with buttery-colored chanterelle mushrooms. They taste delicious in soups, pastas, and stews, but I love to put them on a culinary pedestal.

Simply sautéed and piled atop a wedge of brie—but camembert, or any cheese that threatens to be gooey, will work—the mushroom slices look like little jewels. Choose the smallest chanterelles for this recipe, and slice any tough ends off. If you're uncertain how to choose chanterelles, buy them at Sosio's Produce, where co-owner Mike Osborn, a mushroom specialist, is always happy to help.

Serve the brie with hearty crackers or toasts—just make sure they're strong enough to hold up to a good smearing of cheese.

active time **10 minutes** | *makes* **4 appetizer servings**

½ pound wedge brie cheese
1 tablespoon unsalted butter
¼ pound chanterelle mushrooms, rinsed, trimmed, and sliced into ¼-inch strips
Kosher salt and freshly ground black pepper
1 tablespoon chopped fresh parsley

- Place the brie on a serving plate and bring to room temperature.

- Melt the butter in a large skillet over medium-high heat. When it begins to sizzle, add the mushrooms, and season to taste with salt and pepper. Sauté for 3 to 5 minutes, or until the mushrooms have given up their water and the water has evaporated. Stir in the parsley, pile the mushrooms on top of the cheese, and serve immediately, with crackers or toasts.

WILD MUSHROOM TAGLIATELLE

recipe by **Mike Easton, of Lecosho**

At Lecosho, the restaurant south of the Market opened by Matt Janke, formerly of Matt's in the Market, the wild mushroom ragù is made with whatever's in season—chanterelles in the fall, followed by black trumpet mushrooms as winter draws near, and morels in the spring. For dinner, he serves it with house-made pasta, like his farro tagliatelle, which is made with local emmer flour. This home cook–friendly version uses store-bought pasta and chanterelles, which the Pike Place Market usually has all fall. Feel free to substitute whichever wild mushrooms are in season.

Serve the pasta with a big green salad or Shredded White Winter Salad with Endive, Pears, and Blue Cheese (page 40).

active time **40 minutes** | *makes* **4 servings**

¼ cup plus 2 tablespoons (¾ stick) unsalted butter, divided
3 cloves garlic, finely chopped
2 large shallots, finely chopped
1 pound chanterelle mushrooms, rinsed, trimmed, and sliced
Kosher salt and freshly ground black pepper
¾ pound tagliatelle, fettuccini, or linguine
¼ cup dry white wine
⅓ cup vegetable broth
½ cup heavy cream
2 teaspoons chopped fresh thyme
Grated Parmesan cheese, for serving

- Bring a large pot of water to a boil for the pasta.

- Melt ¼ cup of the butter in a large saucepan or soup pot over medium-low heat. When melted, add the garlic and shallots, and cook for 2 to 3 minutes, stirring occasionally, or until they begin to soften. Add the mushrooms, season to taste with salt and pepper, and cook until they begin to lose their water, 3 to 5 minutes. Increase heat to high and cook for 2 minutes, or until the liquid has almost evaporated.

- Start cooking the pasta according to package instructions.

- Add the wine to the mushrooms and cook for 3 to 5 minutes over medium-high heat, or until most of the liquid has evaporated. Add the broth, bring to a simmer, reduce the heat to low, and cook for 2 minutes. Add the cream and the remaining 2 tablespoons butter, and continue cooking until the sauce has thickened, stirring occasionally. Season to taste with salt and pepper, and stir in the thyme.

- When the pasta is done, drain and toss with the mushroom sauce. Serve immediately, garnished liberally with Parmesan.

SHREDDED WHITE WINTER SALAD
with ENDIVE, PEARS, *and* BLUE CHEESE

Too often, we think of salads in strict terms: green leafy things, tomato, avocado. Made with bitter endive, chopped winter pears, rich blue cheese, and toasted nuts, this shredded salad may redefine your idea of it as a summer food. For a healthy, slightly fancy appetizer, buy an extra endive or two and keep a few of the pretty middle leaves of each endive whole. Pile the finished salad into the endive spears and serve.

You can whisk together the vinaigrette ahead, but because endive and pears tend to brown when exposed to air, it's best to make this salad just before serving.

At the Pike Place Market, look for locally made Willapa Hills Farmstead blue cheese at Beecher's Handmade Cheese or visit Quality Cheese for an excellent selection from around the world.

active time **30 minutes** | *makes* **6 servings**

1 recipe Basic French Vinaigrette (page 186)

1 tablespoon freshly squeezed lemon juice

1 pound (about 6 medium) endive, ends trimmed

1 large red pear

4 ounces blue cheese, crumbled

¼ cup toasted nuts, such as walnuts, pecans, or pine nuts, chopped (optional)

- Whisk the vinaigrette and the lemon juice to blend in a small bowl and set aside.

- Slice the endive across the core into ¼-inch strips (or shred with the shredding disc of a food processor) and toss immediately with the vinaigrette to prevent browning. Slice the pear into similar-size pieces (skinny 1-inch batons) and add to the endive, along with the blue cheese and nuts. Toss to coat with the vinaigrette (you may not use it all) and serve immediately.

BRAISED BABY BACK RIBS
with CHIPOTLE-CHERRY SAUCE

Chukar Cherries' dried bings are delicious eaten out of hand or stirred into oatmeal cookies, but since they're so sweet, they're also a great addition to barbecue sauce. These ribs, made with a pepper-spiked sauce that mellows while the ribs braise in it, can be made ahead of time—just cool and refrigerate the ribs before reheating them for 10 minutes at 450°F when it's time to eat.

active time **40 minutes** | *makes* **4 to 6 servings**

4½ pounds baby back ribs (two 2¼-pound racks or similar)

2 teaspoons canola oil

1 medium onion, chopped

3 to 5 chipotle peppers in adobo sauce

8 ounces (1½ cups) dried bing cherries

3 cloves garlic, crushed

1 (28-ounce) can crushed tomatoes

⅔ cup apple cider vinegar

½ teaspoon kosher salt

¼ cup (packed) light brown sugar

- Transfer the ribs to a large roasting pan or a high-sided baking sheet covered with aluminum foil. (It's OK if the ribs overlap a little.) Pat them dry with paper towels and set aside for about 20 minutes, so they come to room temperature.

- Preheat the oven to 300°F.

- Heat a large saucepan over medium heat. Add the oil, then the onions, and cook, stirring occasionally, until they begin to soften, about 5 minutes. Stir in the chipotles, cherries, garlic, tomatoes, vinegar, salt, and brown sugar. Bring the mixture to a simmer, then reduce heat and cook at a bare simmer for about 20 minutes, until the cherries are soft. In a food processor or blender, puree the sauce until smooth and season with additional salt or adobo sauce, if desired. (The spice will mellow a bit while the ribs bake.)

- Turn the ribs bone side up. Slather them with about a third of the sauce, then turn them over. Coat the meaty side of the ribs with about half the remaining sauce (it will seem like a ton of sauce, but you're basically braising the ribs), allowing it to fall down the sides and surround the meat. Cover the pan tightly with aluminum foil and set the unused sauce aside in a small saucepan. Bake the ribs for 75 to 90 minutes, until the meat shrinks away from the bones and the ribs pull apart easily. Remove from the oven. (You can also grill the ribs.)

- Increase the oven temperature to 450°F. Using tongs and a small knife, cut the ribs into 4-rib sections and transfer them to a large baking dish, meaty side up. (It's OK if they overlap.) Using a big brush or sauce mop, smear some of the thicker sauce from the baking sheet over the ribs. Roast for 15 minutes more, or until the sauce has thickened and the ribs are slightly darker along their edges. While the ribs roast, gently reheat the reserved sauce. Serve the ribs hot, with extra sauce for dipping.

PROFILE: *Pam Montgomery, Chukar Cherries*

In the mid-1980s, Chukar Cherries founder Pam Montgomery left a successful marketing career in Seattle and moved her family to an 8,000-tree cherry orchard in Washington's fertile Yakima Valley. After a few years and a lot of tinkering, Pam decided the conventional wisdom that cherries couldn't be dried without sugar and artificial preservatives was wrong—and launched Chukar Cherries, named for the fleeting red-legged game bird that inhabits the arid Horse Heaven Hills flanking the region. Today, at the Pike Place Market and its flagship store in Prosser, Washington, Chukar Cherries is renowned for naturally dried and chocolate-covered cherries that put the old-school boxed variety to shame. At home, Pam loves baking with Chukar dried tart cherries. Don't miss the peach-cherry salsa.

ROSEMARY-CRUSTED PORK LOIN
with BALSAMIC RED PLUM SAUCE

You haven't seen plums until you've seen what Tiny's Organic grows. Selling outside on the Pike Place Market's cobblestones in the summer, Tiny's—whose farm in Wenatchee, Washington, is famous for its stone fruits—sells seven varieties of plums alone. Although any of them will work for this deep red sweet-sour sauce, the Santa Rosa variety, usually available in early August, is exceptionally delicious.

For a complete dinner, serve with Herb-Roasted Red Potatoes (page 187) and a big green salad.

active time **30 minutes** | *makes* **6 servings**

for the **pork**

1 (2½-pound) pork loin roast, excess fat trimmed

2 tablespoons olive oil, divided

1 tablespoon finely chopped fresh rosemary

½ cup plain bread crumbs

Kosher salt and freshly ground black pepper

for the **sauce**

3 large (about 1 pound) firm-ripe plums, halved and pitted, then chopped

1 large clove garlic, crushed

1 teaspoon finely chopped fresh rosemary

½ cup balsamic vinegar

2 tablespoons sugar

Kosher salt and freshly ground black pepper

- Preheat the oven to 425°F.

- Place the pork in a small roasting pan, fat side up. Rub the top with about ½ tablespoon of the olive oil. In a small bowl, mix the remaining 1½ tablespoons olive oil, rosemary, and bread crumbs until the crumbs are evenly moist, and season to taste with salt and pepper. Pat the bread crumbs onto the pork, coating it in an even layer on the top and sides, and slide it into the oven on the middle rack. Roast for 40 to 50 minutes, or until the top is brown and the center of the roast measures 140°F with an instant-read thermometer. (If the top begins to brown too quickly, slide a baking sheet onto the rack above the pork or cover the pork with aluminum foil.)

- Meanwhile, whirl the plums, garlic, rosemary, balsamic vinegar, sugar, and salt and pepper to taste in a food processor or blender until smooth. Transfer the mixture to a saucepan, bring to a boil, then simmer over low heat for 15 minutes, stirring occasionally. Set aside.

- When the pork is done, let it rest for 5 to 10 minutes as you rewarm the plum sauce over low heat. Slice the pork into 1-inch-thick slabs and serve with the sauce.

PROSCIUTTO-WRAPPED CHICKEN
with APPLES, GORGONZOLA, *and* WHOLE GRAIN MUSTARD CREAM

We know an apple a day keeps the doctor away, but Washington grows enough apple varieties that sometimes it feels like we need a doctorate to choose one. At the Market, get to know the high stall purveyors: for this recipe, ask for an apple that's tart but not too firm, because you don't want it to poke through the tender meat as the chicken cooks. At a supermarket, choose Granny Smith or Pink Lady apples.

active time **45 minutes** | *makes* **4 servings**

4 boneless, skinless chicken breasts (1½ to 2 pounds total), trimmed
Kosher salt and freshly ground black pepper
1 medium tart apple, peeled, cored, and very thinly sliced
¼ pound gorgonzola cheese, crumbled
8 thin slices prosciutto
1 tablespoon olive oil
½ cup heavy cream
2 tablespoons whole grain mustard

- Preheat the oven to 400°F.

- Using a small, sharp knife, cut each chicken breast in half horizontally, keeping one long side intact so the chicken breast opens like a book. Season the chicken to taste with salt and pepper inside and out. Arrange about a quarter of the apple slices (they will overlap) and a quarter of the gorgonzola on the inside half of one chicken breast, and press to close. Place two prosciutto slices on a clean work surface side by side, so they overlap by about ½ inch, and place the chicken in the center of the prosciutto, smooth side up. Wrap the prosciutto up and around the chicken, pressing on the top side so it adheres to itself and encloses the chicken. Repeat with the remaining ingredients.

- Heat a large ovenproof skillet over medium-high heat. When hot, add the olive oil. Swirl the pan to coat, then add the chicken, smooth side down. Cook for 5 to 7 minutes, or until the chicken releases easily from the pan. Carefully turn each piece (it's easiest if you use tongs to pick the chicken up on the cut side) and transfer the pan to the oven. Bake for 10 to 12 minutes, or until the chicken is cooked through.

- Transfer the chicken to a serving platter and return the pan to the stove over high heat. (Careful, the handle will be hot.) Add the cream and mustard to the pan, stir, and cook at a strong simmer until the cream has reduced and thickened, about 2 minutes. Drizzle the sauce over the chicken and serve immediately.

MARKET TIP: *Having Prosciutto Sliced*

Because everyone's idea of "really thin" differs, be specific—for this recipe, ask the butcher to cut the prosciutto to the thickness of two pieces of paper, so it's thin enough to bend easily but thick enough to form a crust around the meat.

FRENCH-STYLE APPLE CUSTARD CAKE

After living in Paris in college, I decided my favorite French dessert was clafouti, the custardy dessert typically made with whole cherries. Although it's sometimes more like a pudding, made without flour, and sometimes more cake-like, it's always an easy, rustic way to use fruit without covering its flavor, and it's always comforting. At Café Campagne, the Market's best place for French comfort food, there's often a clafouti on the menu.

Because clafouti (pronounced cla-foo-TEE) is an intimidating word–the opposite of its effect on the psyche–people avoid making it at home. So I've called this a "French-style apple custard cake." Arrange thinly sliced heirloom apples single file, like housing shingles, and you'll get a cake that's as enjoyable to look at as it is to eat.

Slicing the apples with a mandoline or in a food processor fitted with the slicing blade makes the chopping go more quickly.

active time **30 minutes** | *makes* **one 8-by-8-inch cake**

3 large tart apples (such as Bramley's Seedling, Cox's Orange Pippin, or Granny Smith, about 1½ pounds total)

⅓ cup sugar, plus 2 tablespoons for dusting the cake

3 large eggs

¼ cup all-purpose flour

¼ teaspoon ground cinnamon

¼ teaspoon kosher salt

½ cup heavy cream

½ cup whole milk

½ teaspoon vanilla extract

⅛ teaspoon almond extract

- Preheat the oven to 375°F. Butter an 8-by-8-inch baking dish (or similar) and set aside. (Although a glass dish will work, a ceramic dish is prettiest.)

- Peel and halve the apples, and use a melon baller or a small spoon to scoop out the seeds. Cut the apples into ⅛-inch-thick slices. Place the apples in the prepared pan, arranging them one on top of another, like housing shingles, in three single file lines across the pan; if you're using a round pan, arrange them in a spiral pattern.

- In a medium bowl, whisk ⅓ cup of the sugar with the eggs until the mixture is lighter in color and thick, about 100 strokes. Add the flour, cinnamon, and salt, and whisk to blend. Add the cream, milk, vanilla, and almond extract, and whisk until smooth. Tap the bowl on the counter a few times to release any bubbles, then pour the batter over the apples, making sure it coats them all briefly before sinking down into the pan. Use your hands to pat the apples down, making sure they're evenly submerged.

- Bake the cake for 35 to 40 minutes, or until it is puffed and firm in the center. Let cool for 10 to 20 minutes. About 5 minutes before serving, preheat the oven's broiler on high. Sprinkle the cake with the remaining 2 tablespoons sugar and broil it about 4 inches from the heating unit for just 1 or 2 minutes, watching continuously and turning occasionally, until the tops of the apple slices are caramelized, then serve.

SPICED APRICOT TARTE TATIN

Tarte tatin is typically an upside-down apple tart, made by caramelizing apples in a pan and baking them with the crust on top, then inverting the whole shebang. This version takes advantage of Washington's abundance of great apricots, which color the Market's outdoor farm tables like swathes of fire each summer. The crust, made with heavy cream instead of water, is almost biscuit-like, which makes it perfect for soaking up a drizzle of warm cream at the end.

Out of season, you can replace the apricots with peeled, quartered apples, but don't substitute other stone fruits if they're juicy–too much juice will ruin the caramel.

active time **30 minutes** | *makes* **one 10-inch tart**

for the **pastry**

1¼ cups all-purpose flour
¼ teaspoon kosher salt
½ cup (1 stick) cold unsalted butter, cut into 16 pieces
⅓ cup plus 1 to 2 tablespoons cold heavy cream

for the **filling**

2 tablespoons all-purpose flour
⅛ teaspoon ground cardamom
⅛ teaspoon ground ginger
⅛ teaspoon ground cinnamon
⅛ teaspoon ground cloves
¾ cup plus 2 tablespoons sugar
1½ pounds (about 10 medium) firm-ripe apricots, pitted and quartered
¼ cup water
¼ cup (½ stick) unsalted butter, cut into small pieces, at room temperature

- First, make the pastry: In a large mixing bowl, whisk the flour and salt to blend. Add the butter, pressing it into the flour using your fingertips or a pastry cutter, until the mixture looks like clumpy sand with pea-size bits of butter in it. Drizzle ⅓ cup of the cold cream into the butter/flour mixture a little at a time, using a big fork to mix the ingredients together. Mix and mash until no flour remains at the bottom of the bowl, adding another 1 or 2 tablespoons of cream, as needed.

- Knead the dough 3 or 4 times in the bowl, until it comes together, then form into a rough ball. Transfer the dough onto a sheet of waxed paper, top with another sheet, and roll it out between the two into a roughly 10-inch circle. Transfer the paper-lined dough to a baking sheet and refrigerate at least 30 minutes, or overnight.

- Preheat the oven to 400°F.

- Next, make the filling: In a large bowl, stir together the flour, cardamom, ginger, cinnamon, cloves, and 2 tablespoons of the sugar. Add the apricots and stir to coat the fruit evenly. Set aside.

- Stir the remaining ¾ cup sugar together with the water in a medium ovenproof skillet. Bring to a simmer over high heat and cook, swirling the pan occasionally if the mixture browns in only one spot, until it caramelizes and turns a rich brown color, about 6 minutes. Remove the pan from the heat and scatter the butter pieces around the pan. Stir until all of the butter is melted and incorporated.

- When the foam subsides, arrange the apricots cut side down in the caramel, in a spiral pattern, if desired. Sprinkle any remaining flour mixture over the top. Peel one layer of waxed paper off the crust, then invert the chilled pastry onto the fruit. Peel the other layer off, gently fold any wayward pastry edges under, then slide the pan immediately into the oven. Bake for 25 to 30 minutes, or until the pastry is golden brown. Let cool 10 minutes, then use a small flexible spatula to loosen the pastry from the edges of the pan. Place a serving platter over the pan, then carefully invert both, so the contents of the pan fall onto the plate. (You may have to jiggle the pan a bit to get all the apricots out.) Rearrange any stray apricots, if necessary.

- Let the tart cool for at least 30 minutes, so the caramel firms up, then serve, alone or with ice cream or whipped cream.

TART CHERRY CHOCOLATE CHUNK OATMEAL COOKIES

In college, my friend Peter's grandmother used to send him oatmeal cookies packed in an empty Quaker Oats container, so the other students wouldn't raid his cookie stash. The woman is brilliant, both because of her packaging prowess and because she firmly believes that the gentleman on the top of the Quaker Oats container has the best recipe for oatmeal cookies. You'll find the basis for this recipe under the lid (as "Vanishing Oatmeal Raisin Cookies"), but what his recipe doesn't say is that it's almost infinitely alterable–I add whole wheat flour, big chunks of dark chocolate that make the cookies irresistibly gooey when they're still warm, and Chukar Cherries' dried tart cherries, which beat raisins by a mile in chew and tartness.

active time **20 minutes** | *makes* **about 3 dozen cookies**

1 cup (2 sticks) unsalted butter, at room temperature
¾ cup (packed) light brown sugar
¾ cup sugar
2 large eggs
1 teaspoon vanilla extract
1 cup all-purpose flour
½ cup white whole wheat flour
1 teaspoon baking soda
½ teaspoon kosher salt
2 cups old-fashioned oats
1½ cups dark chocolate chunks (from ½ pound chocolate)
1 cup dried tart cherries (see Note)

- Preheat the oven to 350°F. Line two baking sheets with parchment paper or silicon baking mats and set aside.

- In the work bowl of a stand mixer fitted with the paddle attachment (or using a hand mixer), cream the butter and sugars together on medium speed for about 3 minutes, until light. With the mixer on low, add the eggs one at a time, blending until incorporated between additions and scraping the sides of the bowl if necessary. Stir in the vanilla.

- Meanwhile, whisk the all-purpose and whole wheat flours, baking soda, and salt together in a medium bowl. Add this to the work bowl and mix on low speed until the flour is just incorporated. Add the oats, chocolate, and cherries, and mix well.

- Use an ice cream scoop to portion walnut-size knobs of cookie dough onto the baking sheets, about 12 per sheet, and bake until golden brown at the edges and set in the center, 12 to 15 minutes. Cool 10 minutes on the baking sheets, then transfer to wire racks to cool completely. Repeat with the remaining dough.

NOTE: Some stores sell dried tart cherries as dried "sour" cherries.

MARKET TIP: *Freezing Cookie Dough*

To save cookies for later but still get the fresh-baked effect, place formed cookies on a baking sheet and freeze until firm. Pack the frozen dough into a zip-top bag and freeze for up to 2 months. Bake from frozen as directed, for 15 to 17 minutes.

HOW 'BOUT THEM APPLES?

According to the Washington Apple Commission, the state harvests upward of ten *billion* apples each year, making it Washington's largest agricultural product. And it's no wonder—with a seemingly endless array of varieties and a good shelf life, apples are America's favorite fruit.

We're all familiar with Red Delicious and Granny Smith. But at the Pike Place Market, especially during the fall harvest season, you'll find many more varieties, ranging from Galas and Fujis to varieties that are less well known, like Cripps Pink, a tart and tangy variety with a good snap, loved by snackers and bakers alike. Increasingly, Seattleites are buying heirloom apples. Next time you hit the market, look for a cameo appearance of one of these unique varieties.

BELLE DE BOSKOOP These red apples often have a slightly tough, russet-tinted top skin that makes them best for baking. They're great storage apples, and they get sweeter the longer they're kept—keep them in mind in midwinter.

BRAMLEY'S SEEDLING A British classic, this firm, tart apple is great for baking because it holds its shape well.

CALVILLE BLANC D'HIVER This is an exceptionally sweet apple; use it for sauces and juice, or for pie, if you want to cut back on the processed sugar.

COX'S ORANGE PIPPIN Pale green with red stripes, this is a great all-around apple—tart, firm flesh makes it good for baking, but it's tender enough to eat out of hand.

GOLDEN RUSSET They're not the prettiest, but you might be surprised by how juicy these nutty-flavored apples are. Great for applesauce.

GRAVENSTEIN These red- and orange-marbled gems don't last long, but when they're ripe, early in the apple season, use them in pies; they have a strong, complex flavor.

MACOUN A cross between a McIntosh and a Jersey Black, this apple has the McIntosh's green-blushed top, tart flavor, and propensity to do well over the winter—but it's not the best choice for a pie. Peel it and eat it smeared with nut butter.

10 WAYS ► *with Apples*

APPLE, HAM, *and* CHEDDAR OMELET
Try an omelet made with peeled, cubed tart apples; chopped black forest ham; and shredded sharp cheddar (such as Beecher's Flagship).

CURRIED CHICKEN SALAD *with* APPLES *and* COCONUT
Blend 2 teaspoons curry powder with a 7-ounce container plain Greek yogurt, 2 tablespoons mayonnaise, salt and pepper to taste, ¼ cup chopped basil, a shredded apple, and ½ cup toasted coconut. Stir in 2 cooked, shredded chicken breasts, and pile into pita bread.

APPLE-CRANBERRY SAUCE *with* CINNAMON *and* ROSEMARY
Simmer 1 (10-ounce) bag fresh or frozen cranberries with 1 chopped, peeled tart apple, 1 cup sugar, ½ cup water, 1 large sprig fresh rosemary, 1 teaspoon ground cinnamon, and a pinch of salt over low heat, until the berries burst and the sauce thickens, about an hour.

APPLES *with* GOAT CHEESE–PECAN DIP
In a food processor, whirl ½ cup chopped, toasted pecans with 4 ounces softened goat cheese, ¼ cup heavy cream, and salt and pepper to taste. Use as a dip for tart apple wedges.

SQUASH *and* APPLE SOUP
Roast a 4-pound squash and scoop the flesh out. Sauté onions in a soup pot in olive oil and butter until soft, then add the squash; 2 peeled, chopped tart apples; and chicken or vegetable broth to cover. Simmer until all ingredients are soft, then puree until smooth. Season to taste with ground ginger, maple syrup, salt, and pepper.

APPLES *with* CINNAMON CREAM CHEESE

The perfect lunchbox snack: slice and core an apple with a dedicated apple slicer. Toss the core, put the apple back together, and stuff the core space with cream cheese seasoned with ground cinnamon and sugar.

RED WINTER SALAD

Make the Shredded White Winter Salad with Endive, Pears, and Blue Cheese (page 40), replacing the endive with 2 heads of radicchio (shredded) and the pears with tart red-skinned apples.

GRILLED PORK CHOPS *with* CARAMELIZED APPLES *and* ONIONS

Slice a tart apple and a small onion crosswise through the core, picking any seeds out of the apple. Coat the apple and onion slices and 4 pork chops with olive oil, salt, pepper, and chopped fresh thyme to taste. Grill over high heat, putting the onions on the grill with the pork chops and adding the apples when they are both ready to flip, brushing all with apple cider during the last minute of cooking.

HOT APPLE-RHUBARB COMPOTE

Simmer 1 pound peeled, chopped Pink Lady apples with 1 pound chopped rhubarb, ½ cup apple cider, and ¼ cup sugar for 20 minutes, or until the rhubarb begins to fall apart. Serve over ice cream, mascarpone cheese, or Greek yogurt.

APPLE-BLACKBERRY CRISP

Blend 3 peeled, chopped apples; 2 cups frozen blackberries; 2 tablespoons flour; and ½ cup sugar; bake at 375°F for 20 minutes. Mix ½ cup each flour, old-fashioned oats, brown sugar, chopped nuts, and melted butter with ½ teaspoon ground cinnamon, scatter on top of the apples and berries, and bake for another 30 minutes, until browned and bubbling.

FROM *the* GARDEN

RECIPE LIST

HIGH STALLS: *Is This Produce Local?*

The Pike Place Market's produce purveyors fall into two categories: they're either day-stall tenants, who rent space from the Market on a day-to-day basis and sell their own locally produced crops from tables, or high-stall tenants. The latter are full, permanent commercial businesses, so named because their stalls are typically built around a platform, which raises the vendors up a few feet above customers, and because the produce is often arranged higher than table level, in tiers.

The high-stall system was created in the 1920s, as a response to customers' demands for year-round produce. While day-stallers may only sell foods grown by the farms themselves, high-stallers can use wholesalers from anywhere around the world—hence the constant abundance of, say, watermelon in the wintertime. Not surprisingly, the number of day-stallers selling produce is much greater in the summer than in the winter.

However, over the past few decades, as shoppers have become more conscious of using locally produced foods, high-stallers have developed niches—Sosio's Produce, for example, is known for its assortment of local wild mushrooms, while Frank's Quality Produce is known to chefs throughout Seattle for its greens, like arugula and butter lettuce. Choice Produce—now Choice Produce & Pepper—is best for peppers and pepper products. And all of them are consistently good at pointing out which foods have been sourced locally.

But while the high stalls may sell many of the fruits and vegetables you can find in your local grocery store, they survive by tending to rituals absent in today's supermarkets. Each morning, the displays are lovingly built; the people bagging your produce can tell you which grapefruit is best because they've actually looked at each one. When customers approach, high-stallers are often seen sampling out the day's best produce, teaching customers about Taylor's Gold pears or green zebra tomatoes, or something else they might not recognize. Buying produce is an intensely personal process.

So no, the Pike Place Market's produce isn't all local—only the produce on the low day-stall tables was grown by the people selling it. But it's all loved.

SALADE VERTE

recipe by **Jim Drohman, of Le Pichet**

If there's one best way to treat a head of perfect butter lettuce from Frank's Quality Produce, it's the way they do it at Le Pichet, the timeless little French bistro near the corner of First and Virginia. Bathe it gently, then chill it in the fridge. Just before lunch, stack the crisp leaves up in a little mountain on a cold plate, then dress them with a delicate hazelnut vinaigrette, sharp with sherry vinegar and Dijon mustard and sweet with orange juice. Shower them with freshly toasted hazelnuts–chef Jim Drohman swears by the Market's Holmquist Hazelnut Orchards' DuChilly variety, because they have really thin skins–and dig in.

This recipe makes four main-course lunch portions but would serve six or eight as the start to a larger meal.

active time **25 minutes** | *makes* **4 servings**

1 cup freshly squeezed orange juice (from 3 oranges)
1 small shallot, roughly chopped
⅓ cup toasted whole hazelnuts, plus ½ cup toasted and roughly chopped
½ cup sherry vinegar
1 tablespoon Dijon mustard
Kosher salt and freshly ground black pepper
½ cup soy or canola oil (or to taste)
1 large head butter lettuce, washed and chilled

- In a small saucepan, bring the orange juice to a simmer over medium heat. Cook until the juice has reduced to about ½ cup, then cool.

- Just before serving, combine the cooled juice, shallot, ⅓ cup whole hazelnuts, vinegar, mustard, and salt and pepper to taste in a blender, and whirl on high speed until homogenous. With the blender running, add the oil in a slow, steady stream and blend until the mixture has the consistency of heavy cream–don't overmix, as the vinaigrette will break if it gets too warm. Season to taste with additional salt, pepper, and oil, as needed.

- Core the lettuce and separate it into leaves, tearing them in two if they are larger than the palm of your hand. Toss the lettuce with salt and pepper to taste, and a little vinaigrette. (You won't use it all, and it's important not to overdress this salad.) Arrange the lettuce on individual plates (or one big platter), and sprinkle the chopped hazelnuts over the top. Serve immediately.

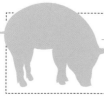

MARKET TIP: *Toasting Nuts*

To toast nuts, place them on a sheet pan and roast for 10 to 15 minutes at 350°F, until browned and fragrant. In the case of hazelnuts, the nuts are cool enough to use when they stop making crackling noises.

THREE GIRLS' GAZPACHO

recipe by **Atarah Levy, of Three Girls Bakery**

Jack and Atarah Levy, the husband-wife team behind Three Girls Bakery, have made a name for themselves selling great breads, pastries, and sandwiches from a tiny storefront right on Pike Place. I can eat their poppy seed rugelach any time of day, any day, but during Seattle's gray winters, I crave their gazpacho, which blends all my favorite quintessential summer garden ingredients into one perfect bowl. Start with the corn, tomatoes, peppers, onions, and cucumbers listed here, then be imaginative—try adding halved yellow cherry tomatoes, steamed green beans, chopped jalapeños, or whatever else appeals to you.

active time **40 minutes** | *makes* **6 servings**

2 large cucumbers, peeled, seeded, and chopped

4 cups tomato juice, divided

3 ears whole corn, cooked, then cut off the cob in large chunks (see page 78 for an easy corn-cutting technique)

2 ripe avocados, halved, pitted, peeled, and chopped

2 large ripe tomatoes, seeded and chopped

½ medium red onion, finely chopped

1 bell pepper (any color), stemmed, seeded, and chopped

2 cloves garlic, very finely chopped or pressed

½ cup chopped fresh cilantro, plus more for serving

1 large lemon

Tabasco sauce (or other hot pepper sauce)

Kosher salt and freshly ground black pepper

Honey

Sour cream, for serving

- In a blender or food processor, puree one of the cucumbers with 1 cup of the tomato juice. Transfer to a large mixing bowl, and add the remaining 3 cups tomato juice, remaining cucumber, corn, avocado, tomato, onion, bell pepper, garlic, and cilantro. Squeeze the lemon's juice over everything, then stir and season to taste with Tabasco (6 to 12 dashes to start), salt and pepper, and honey, if the mixture tastes too acidic to you. Here, you can tinker, adding other ingredients, or more tomato juice, if you want a soupier texture. Serve topped with sour cream and additional chopped cilantro, if desired.

- The soup may be made up to 2 days ahead and stored, covered in the refrigerator, until ready to serve. (The flavor actually improves with time.)

ROASTED PICKLED CAULIFLOWER SALAD

recipe by **Dale Nelson, of Woodring Northwest Specialties**

Woodring Northwest Specialties is a taste-tester's paradise. From preserves and marmalades to chocolate and caramel sauces, every spoonful brings a burst of new flavor. My personal favorite, though, is Woodring's pickle selection, especially the pickled asparagus. At home, the affable Dale Nelson, who runs the business with his wife, dabbles in pickles that are much less ordinary. This striking salad combines a spicy pickled cauliflower with fennel and onion—it's the perfect conversation piece if you're asked to bring a salad to dinner.

Fennel fronds are the green, feathery tops attached to a fennel bulb; for instructions on how to handle fennel, see page 78.

active time **35 minutes** | *makes* **4 to 6 servings**

for the **roasted cauliflower**

1 large head cauliflower, cut into bite-size florets
2 tablespoons extra-virgin olive oil
Kosher salt and freshly ground black pepper

for the **pickling brine**

1 cup warm water
2 tablespoons sugar
1 tablespoon kosher salt
1 teaspoon crushed red pepper flakes
2 cloves garlic, minced
1 cup white wine vinegar
½ cup fennel fronds

for the **dressing**

1 teaspoon Dijon mustard
1 teaspoon minced garlic
2 tablespoons orange juice
2 tablespoons white wine vinegar
½ cup extra-virgin olive oil
Kosher salt and freshly ground black pepper

- Preheat the oven to 400°F. Line a baking sheet with parchment paper or a silicon baking mat, and set aside.

- Place the cauliflower in a large bowl, drizzle with the olive oil, and season to taste with salt and pepper. Stir the cauliflower to coat each floret well, then transfer to the prepared baking sheet. Roast the cauliflower until lightly browned, about 20 minutes. Transfer the cauliflower to a bowl and allow to cool completely.

- While the cauliflower cools, make the pickling brine: Stir the water, sugar, salt, red pepper flakes, and garlic together in a large pickling jar (or a similar container that can hold all the florets) until the sugar and salt dissolve. Add the white wine vinegar and the fennel fronds.

- When the cauliflower has cooled to room temperature, add it to the pickling brine, and refrigerate overnight.

for the salad

¼ cup toasted hazelnuts, coarsely
    chopped
1 small bulb fennel, very thinly sliced
1 small sweet onion, very thinly sliced
3 cups mixed salad greens
Freshly ground black pepper

- Make the dressing: In a small bowl, whisk together the mustard, garlic, orange juice, and vinegar. While whisking, add the olive oil in a slow, steady stream, whisking until emulsified. Season to taste with salt and pepper.

- To serve the salad, mix together about a cup of the pickled cauliflower (drained) with the hazelnuts, fennel, onion, and salad greens. Add dressing to taste and serve immediately, garnished with pepper.

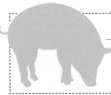

MARKET TIP: *Dressing for Dinner*

To prepare a salad ahead of time without risking soggy lettuce, place the dressing in the bottom of a serving bowl, then add the crunchy ingredients. Add the lettuce last, and toss the salad just before serving.

FRESH FALL HOT-AND-SOUR SOUP

This is not traditional Chinese hot-and-sour soup, but it was born close by. Down an easily forgotten staircase near City Fish—the Market's oldest fish shop—Pike Place Chinese Cuisine serves fantastic fare with an astounding view of the Sound. Start your market trip with a bowl of its pork-studded soup, then march upstairs to gather ingredients for this brightly hued vegetarian version, which has the same punch of white pepper and vinegar but uses fresh fall farmers' market ingredients, such as mushrooms, kale, squash, and carrots.

Outside of chanterelle season, you can use all shiitake mushrooms.

active time **45 minutes** | *makes* **4 servings**

3 tablespoons cornstarch
3 tablespoons cold water
1 teaspoon sugar
1 tablespoon soy sauce
3 teaspoons dark sesame oil, divided
8 ounces tofu (about ½ package)
3 leaves lacinato (aka dinosaur) kale
1 tablespoon canola oil
2 carrots, peeled and shredded
½ delicata squash, seeded and
  shredded
¼ pound chanterelle mushrooms,
  rinsed, trimmed and thinly sliced
¼ pound shiitake mushrooms, rinsed,
  trimmed, and thinly sliced
6 cups vegetable or mushroom broth
¼ cup plus 1 tablespoon white
  vinegar
½ teaspoon freshly ground white
  pepper
1 large egg, beaten

- In a small bowl, blend the cornstarch, water, sugar, soy sauce, and 2 teaspoons of the sesame oil together with a fork until combined, and set aside.

- Cut the tofu into ¼-inch batons and set aside. Cut the tough ribs out of the kale and slice the leaves horizontally into ¼-inch strips. Set aside.

- Heat a wok or large soup pot over high heat. When hot, add the canola oil and the remaining teaspoon of sesame oil, then the carrots and squash. Cook for 1 minute, stirring, then add the kale and mushrooms. Sauté for 2 minutes, until the kale has wilted. Add the broth, then the tofu, and bring to a simmer. Stir the cornstarch mixture, add it to the soup, and bring the soup back to a simmer, stirring occasionally until it looks a bit thicker and almost glossy. Remove the pan from the heat, stir in the vinegar and pepper, and taste for seasoning—you'll probably want a bit more vinegar and/or pepper. Stir the mixture around in a circle once or twice, creating a gentle whirlpool. Stop stirring and drizzle the egg into the swirling liquid—it will cook upon contact in long, thin strings. Serve immediately.

THREE GREENS TART *with* GOAT CHEESE *and* PINE NUTS

One of the Pike Place Market's downsides–if you could call it that–is that produce is displayed so beautifully, it's often difficult to come home with only what's on your list. This tart takes advantage of fresh spinach, red chard, and lacinato kale (the thin, dark green kind also known as dinosaur kale), which means your bag will be bursting before you're too tempted. It travels well and puts on a good face for company, which makes it a great option for potlucks and parties.

The tart is also delicious with about ¼ cup of olive tapenade or pesto spread under the goat cheese. Use the remaining greens to make Simple Sautéed Greens (page 188).

active time **45 minutes** | *makes* **one 10-by-15-inch tart**

1 tablespoon extra-virgin olive oil
1 large onion, sliced
Kosher salt and freshly ground black
   pepper
1 clove garlic, finely chopped
¼ pound spinach, rinsed and chopped
   (about 2 packed cups chopped)
¼ pound red chard, rinsed, tough ribs
   removed, and chopped (about 2
   packed cups chopped)
¼ pound dinosaur kale, rinsed, tough
   ribs removed, and chopped (about
   2 packed cups chopped)
⅓ cup toasted pine nuts
1 (10-by-15-inch, or similar) sheet puff
   pastry, thawed overnight in the
   refrigerator
8 ounces goat cheese

- Preheat the oven to 400°F. Line a baking sheet with parchment paper or a silicon baking mat and set aside.

- Heat a large skillet over medium heat. Add the oil, then the onion, and season to taste with salt and pepper. Cook, stirring occasionally, until the onions are lightly browned, about 20 minutes. Add the garlic, then the spinach, chard, and kale, and sauté for about 10 minutes, until the greens have lost all their water. Stir in the pine nuts, check seasonings and add more salt or pepper if necessary, and set aside.

- Gently unroll the puff pastry onto the prepared baking sheet, patting any creases smooth. (You can add some pizzazz by pressing the tines of a fork into the crust at 1-inch intervals all the way around the edges.) Crumble the goat cheese all over the dough (don't leave much of a border), and top with the greens mixture.

- Bake the tart for 25 to 30 minutes, or until the edges are deep golden brown. Cool 10 minutes on the pan, then transfer carefully to a platter, slice, and serve.

POTATO *and* PEA SAMOSAS
with MINTED YOGURT DIPPING SAUCE

Cajetan Mendonca, a tall, smiling man from the Indian state of Goa, started Saffron Spice in 2009. His samosas—traditional Indian tetrahedral pastries stuffed with a variety of meats, vegetables, and spices, then deep-fried—come in many flavors, but my favorite is the vegetarian kind, with potatoes and peas. Here's a version made with ingredients available at most large grocery stores. For a party, pair these with mango lemonade.

active time **1 hour** | *makes* **about 20 samosas**

1½ pounds baby red potatoes
1 cup fresh or frozen peas
1 teaspoon whole cumin seeds
½ teaspoon garam masala
½ teaspoon curry powder
½ teaspoon kosher salt
½ cup plain Indian- or Greek-style
   yogurt
3 tablespoons unsalted butter, cut into
   small cubes
1 (16-ounce) package 6-inch egg roll
   wrappers
Canola oil, for frying
2 cups Minted Yogurt Dipping Sauce
   (recipe follows)

- Place the potatoes in a large saucepan and add cold water to cover. Bring to a boil, then simmer until the potatoes can be pierced easily with a fork or wooden skewer, about 15 to 20 minutes, depending on the size of your potatoes.

- Meanwhile, put the peas, cumin seeds, garam masala, curry powder, salt, yogurt, and butter in a large mixing bowl. Add the hot potatoes, and use a potato masher to smash the mixture together until the potatoes are in pieces no bigger than the tip of your thumb. Set aside.

- Fill a small bowl with water and place it near a clean work surface. Working with one egg roll wrapper at a time, place a wrapper on the surface and fold it in half diagonally, so it forms a triangle. Place a scant ¼ cup filling in the center of the triangle. Imagine drawing another triangle inside the wrapper, so that the points of the second intersect the straight parts of the first, and use your hands to pat the filling into this inverted triangle shape. Dip your fingers in the water and paint a thin layer of water on the remaining portion of the egg roll wrapper. Fold each of the three corners up and around the filling, patting any newly exposed wrapper with a few dabs of water as you fold to encourage the subsequent layers to adhere. Pinch the corners closed if the dough doesn't quite cover the filling, and set the samosa aside on a baking sheet. Repeat with the remaining ingredients.

- About halfway through assembling the samosas, add oil to a depth of about ¾ inch in a large, deep skillet and bring it to 350°F (measured with a deep-fat thermometer) over medium heat. Fry the samosas 5 or 6 at a time for about 1 minute per side, or until golden brown. Transfer fried samosas to a paper towel-lined plate and repeat with the remaining ingredients, alternating frying and folding the rest of the samosas. Serve warm, with Minted Yogurt Dipping Sauce.

MINTED YOGURT DIPPING SAUCE

Feel free to tinker with the seasonings–dill works beautifully in place of the mint, and freshly chopped garlic is a delicious addition.

active time **5 minutes** | *makes* **2 cups**

2 cups plain Indian- or Greek-style yogurt
¼ cup finely chopped fresh mint
½ teaspoon ground cumin
Juice of ½ medium lemon (about 1½ tablespoons)
Kosher salt

- Stir the yogurt, mint, cumin, and lemon juice together in a small bowl, and season to taste with salt. Refrigerate until ready to serve.

ALEX'S VEGETABLE CHILI

recipe by **Anthony Polizzi, of Steelhead Diner**

It's hard to convince a devout carnivore that the best chili you've ever tasted had no meat in it. But true to form, the cooks at Steelhead Diner, lead by chef Anthony Polizzi, surprise us with a vegetarian chili that can only be described as transcendent. Inspired by prep cook Alex Diaz, it's a good reminder that branching away from the fish dishes at Steelhead–themselves examples of excellence–isn't necessarily a mistake. Because it starts with dried beans, you'll need to start the chili the day before, but it improves with age, so making it a few days ahead is actually a plus.

The toppings for this chili are unusual–first broiled with a layer of cheese, as if it had had a late-night run-in with a french onion soup, the bowls at Steelhead are dabbed with pico de gallo and a cilantro-spiked sour cream. Follow their lead, or just use your favorite accompaniments.

NOTE: Look for chili sauce near the ketchup in your local grocery store–this recipe calls for a regular glass-bottled American-style sauce, not an Asian chili sauce. Also, feel free to use other seasonal vegetables– mushrooms, carrots, or parsnips, for example–in place of the root vegetables and squash here. In the summer, pile the soup full of fresh peppers from Choice Produce & Pepper.

active time **1 hour 15 minutes** | *makes* **6 to 8 servings**

1¼ cups dried pinto beans
1¼ cups dried red kidney beans
1¼ cups dried black beans
1 small turnip, peeled and cut into
  ½-inch pieces
1 small rutabaga, peeled and cut into
  ½-inch pieces
1 cup chopped (½-inch pieces)
  butternut squash
½ cup canola oil, divided
Kosher salt and freshly ground black
  pepper

continued

- Place all the beans in a 1-gallon nonreactive container. Cover with water by 3 inches, and set aside to soak overnight. Drain.

- Preheat the oven to 350°F. In a large bowl, toss the turnip, rutabaga, and squash with ¼ cup of the canola oil and salt and pepper to taste. Transfer the mixture to a baking sheet and roast for 30 to 40 minutes, or until soft. Set aside.

2 cloves garlic, finely chopped
1 small red bell pepper, stemmed, seeded, and cut into ½-inch pieces
1 small green bell pepper, stemmed, seeded, and cut into ½-inch pieces
1 small red onion, diced
1 small yellow onion, diced
2 bay leaves
2 cups vegetable broth
1 cup chili sauce
1 (15-ounce) can tomato sauce
4 tablespoons Chili Spice (recipe follows)
1 small tomato, cut into ½-inch pieces
½ cup chopped fresh cilantro
½ cup chopped green onions
1½ cups grated pepper jack cheese
Pico de Gallo (recipe follows)
Cilantro Sour Cream (recipe follows)

- Heat the remaining ¼ cup canola oil in a large, heavy-bottomed soup pot with a lid over medium heat until it shimmers. Add the garlic and cook, stirring occasionally, until toasted, 1 to 2 minutes. Add the red and green bell pepper, red and yellow onion, and bay leaves, and cook, stirring occasionally, until the vegetables are soft, about 10 minutes. Add the beans, broth, chili and tomato sauces, and Chili Spice, and stir to combine. Bring the chili to a simmer, then cook over low heat, covered, stirring occasionally, until all the bean varieties are cooked through, about 2½ to 3 hours. (If the chili seems dry, you may need to add a cup or two of water or broth, depending on the size of your vegetables and how loose you like your chili.) Remove the bay leaves.

- About 15 minutes before serving, preheat the broiler. Stir in the reserved roasted vegetables, chopped tomato, cilantro, and green onions. Bring the chili back to a simmer, stir vigorously to break up some of the beans, and adjust the seasoning with salt and perhaps more of the remaining Chili Spice. Transfer the chili to ovenproof bowls (6 large or 8 smaller bowls). Sprinkle the cheese evenly over the chili, place the bowls on a baking sheet, and broil the chili on the middle rack of the oven for a few minutes, until the cheese is melted and bubbling. Serve the chili immediately, topped with dabs of Pico de Gallo and Cilantro Sour Cream.

CHILI SPICE

At the Pike Place Market, look for these spices at El Mercado Latino, World Spice Merchants, or MarketSpice.

active time **5 minutes** | *makes* **about ⅓ cup**

1 tablespoon ground cumin
1 teaspoon ground coriander
1 teaspoon ground white pepper
½ teaspoon ground fennel seed
½ teaspoon ground cinnamon
1 tablespoon guajillo chile powder
1 tablespoon plus 1 teaspoon pasilla
  chile powder
1 tablespoon plus 1 teaspoon ancho
  chile powder

- Mix all ingredients to blend in a small bowl. (Any unused spice can be placed in an airtight container and stored for future use, for flavoring soups or rubbing steaks or chicken before grilling.)

PICO DE GALLO

active time **10 minutes** | *makes* **½ cup**

1 ripe tomato, finely chopped
2 tablespoons finely chopped red onion
2 teaspoons finely chopped serrano
  pepper
2 teaspoons finely chopped fresh
  cilantro
2 teaspoons freshly squeezed lime juice
Kosher salt

- Mix the tomato, onion, pepper, cilantro, and lime juice to blend in a small bowl. Season to taste with salt, and refrigerate until ready to serve.

CILANTRO SOUR CREAM

active time **5 minutes** | *makes* **⅔ cup**

½ cup sour cream
½ cup chopped fresh cilantro
2 teaspoons freshly squeezed lime juice
Kosher salt

- Mix the sour cream, cilantro, and lime juice to blend in a small bowl. Season to taste with salt, and refrigerate until ready to serve.

BRAISED HALIBUT *with* CARAMELIZED FENNEL *and* OLIVES

Served in a white wine-lemon broth with plenty of crunchy bread for mopping up the juices, this simple, quick-braised fish recipe pairs flavors from the Mediterranean with fresh Alaskan halibut fillets. If you'd like, reserve some of the feathery green fennel fronds, chop them, and sprinkle them over the finished dish. (See page 78 for instructions on how to handle fennel.)

NOTE: Castelvetrano olives are the most delicious choice, but they're hard to pit when they're cold, so I leave them whole here. If you don't like eating olives with pits in them, use another pitted green olive. Occasionally, DeLaurenti carries pitted Castelvetranos–call ahead.

active time **45 minutes** | *makes* **4 servings**

1 tablespoon olive oil
2 fennel bulbs (about 1¼ pounds total), halved and cut through the core into 10 or 12 sections
Kosher salt and freshly ground black pepper
1 cup Castelvetrano olives
1 cup dry white wine
2 tablespoons butter, cut into 4 pieces
4 small (1-inch-thick) halibut fillets (about 1½ pounds total), skinned
1 teaspoon chopped fresh oregano
1 lemon, quartered
Bread, for soaking up the juices

- Preheat the oven to 450°F.

- Heat a large ovenproof skillet over medium heat. When hot, add the oil, then the fennel (cut sides down), and season to taste with salt and pepper. Cook for 15 minutes, turning the fennel only twice during cooking, until well caramelized on all sides. Add the olives, wine, and butter, and bring the mixture to a strong simmer. Season the fish with salt, pepper, and the oregano, and nestle the pieces of fish into the fennel and olive mixture. Add the lemon quarters and roast in the oven for 8 to 10 minutes, just until the fish is cooked through.

- Squeeze the hot lemons over the fish and discard. Use a spatula to transfer the fish and fennel to shallow bowls, and spoon the remaining ingredients and broth over the fish. Serve immediately, with bread.

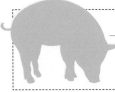

MARKET TIP: *Asking for Help*

More so than in a typical grocery store, the Pike Place Market's purveyors are happy to educate you. If you're not sure what fennel looks like, ask. Also ask fishmongers to trim the skin from your halibut for you–if you want, they'll show you how to do it yourself next time.

ROASTED PANCETTA-WRAPPED ASPARAGUS
with GOAT CHEESE

When it comes to eating your vegetables, this is sort of cheating—it's a dish of asparagus bathed in ultimate luxury. First, the spears get wrapped in paper-thin slices of pancetta (an Italian version of unsmoked bacon that's sold in big spirals, like cinnamon rolls made of pork belly). Then they're sprinkled with a layer of crumbled goat cheese and baked until the pancetta is crisp and the cheese melts. In the spring, some produce stands, like Sosio's, offer a choice between thin and fat asparagus; the bigger spears work best for this recipe.

Ask your butcher to lay the pancetta rounds out so the edges don't touch; they're easier to work with that way.

active time **15 minutes** | *makes* **4 servings**

1 teaspoon olive oil
1 pound (about 20 spears) large
  asparagus, ends trimmed
¼ pound (about 20 slices) thinly
  sliced pancetta
Freshly ground black pepper
3 ounces goat cheese, crumbled

- Preheat the oven to 425°F. Rub the bottom of an ovenproof casserole dish with the olive oil and set aside.

- Cut each piece of asparagus in half, so you have a bunch of roughly 4-inch pieces. Reserve the bottom halves for another use (such as the Spring Frittata with Morels, Asparagus, Peas, and Ramps on page 36 or Mediterranean Pasta Salad with Seven-Grain Orzo on page 95). Place a piece of pancetta on a clean work surface. Position one asparagus tip on the bottom edge of the pancetta, and roll the asparagus up. Transfer to the prepared pan, seam side down, and repeat with the remaining ingredients. Season the asparagus with pepper.

- Roast the asparagus for 10 minutes. Sprinkle the crumbled goat cheese on top, and roast for another 5 minutes or so, until the cheese is soft and the pancetta is beginning to brown. Serve immediately.

PROFILE: *Mike Osborn, Sosio's Produce*

After selling produce for more than twenty years, you could say Mike Osborn, the co-owner of Sosio's Produce, knows his stuff. When he's not ribbing regulars or teaching a new customer how to use sea beans in stir-fries, he's delicately arranging the excellent produce Sosio's has been known for since 1948. Mike excels at explaining to shoppers and passersby how to use less familiar vegetables—specimens such as spiky green romanesco, a cauliflower relative, or spring favorites such as fiddlehead ferns or stinging nettles.

CARROT SOUP *with* CUMIN *and* HONEY

Sometimes, shopping for a small, simple dinner at the Pike Place Market can be overwhelming—there's unavoidable temptation to buy, say, an entire salmon, and take it home for a holiday feast when you're only two for dinner. When you just need something warm and satisfying, make this velvety carrot soup, spiced with cumin, cayenne, and *pimentón de la Vera*—smoked paprika from Spain's La Vera region. Look for the *pimentón* at World Spice Merchants, DeLaurenti, The Spanish Table, or in the spice aisle of a large supermarket, in a red box.

   Minted Yogurt Dipping Sauce (page 68) makes an excellent garnish.

active time **45 minutes** | *makes* **4 servings**

1 tablespoon olive oil
1 large yellow onion, chopped
2 pounds carrots, peeled and chopped
   into 1-inch pieces
Kosher salt and freshly ground black
   pepper
1 teaspoon ground cumin
¼ teaspoon *pimentón de la Vera*
   (smoked Spanish paprika)
Small pinch of cayenne
4 cups chicken or vegetable stock
2 tablespoons honey

- Heat a large, heavy soup pot over medium heat. When hot, add the oil, then the onion, and cook, stirring occasionally, for 8 to 10 minutes, or until the onion is soft. Add the carrots, season to taste with salt and pepper, and cook, covered, for another 10 minutes, stirring once or twice. Stir in the cumin, *pimentón*, and cayenne, then add the broth and bring to a simmer. Reduce the heat to low and cook until the carrots are completely soft, another 10 to 20 minutes.

- Using a blender or food processor, carefully puree the hot soup in small batches and return to the pot. Stir in the honey, then check the seasonings, adding more cayenne or honey to taste. Serve hot.

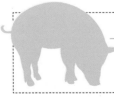

MARKET TIP: *My Favorite Appliance*

An immersion blender—also called a stick blender—is a handheld device that enables you to mix a liquid without transferring it to a blender and back into a pot. It's invaluable for making smooth soups like this one and (my favorite part) takes a lot less time to clean.

THE SUMMER MARKET

Though most of the purveyors explored in this book are at the Market year-round, like any market, Pike Place's stalls explode with fresh seasonal produce when it's warm. Every Wednesday, Saturday, and Sunday, the cobbles of Pike Place itself make way for about thirty additional tenants, and the street turns into a farmers' market called Farm Days on the Cobblestones. Martin Family Orchards sells tree-ripened fruit, Johnson Berry Farm brings in organic berry jams, Magana Farm offers vegetables, and Pipitone Farms has a mixture of all of the above. In fact, in the summer, any farm-table tenant is allowed to pitch his or her own tent directly on Pike Place, selling outdoors instead of in. If only all our offices were so flexible.

Produce Primer

At the Pike Place Market, most of the produce purveyors are excellent at marking locally grown varieties as such—but they're even better at helping shoppers learn to use produce that may be new to them. Don't be shy with the list below: they're all delicious.

ARTICHOKES Although they look thorny and can be time-consuming to prepare if you only want to use the hearts, there's an easy way to steam artichokes for eating: Trim the stem to 1 inch, then cut the spiky top off about 1 inch from its point. Place the artichoke in a microwave-safe bowl filled with 2 inches of water and cover with a microwave-safe plate. Cook on high power for 6 minutes, then let sit, covered, for 20 minutes. Serve with Homemade Aioli (page 184).

BEANS If you're used to canned beans, the dried variety can be intimidating—but the only difficult part of making them is planning ahead. Soak them overnight to help them cook more evenly, then simmer (in new water, if you prefer) until tender, salting about halfway through cooking. (If you salt at the beginning, the skins will get tough.)

BEETS To roast a beet, trim off the greens where they meet the root. Wrap three or four beets together in a package of aluminum foil, place on a baking sheet, and bake at 400°F for 1 hour or so, until a skewer enters the beets with no resistance. Let the beets cool in the package for about 20 minutes—the heat of the vegetable will help loosen the skins—then peel and eat. You can also eat the greens themselves. Use them in Simple Sautéed Greens (page 188) or make beet green chips: Wash and dry the greens from a small bundle of beets, then chop them, toss them with 1 tablespoon olive oil, sprinkle with salt, and roast on a baking sheet (spread out so they don't touch each other) at 325°F for about 20 minutes, until crisp.

CORN We all have our favorite way of eating corn, but cutting it off the cob raw can be challenging. My favorite way: Place a husked corn cob flat on a cutting board, parallel with your knife. Working the long way, cut three rows of corn off at once, then rotate the corn cob away from the knife's blade, and cut another few rows off. Keep cutting until you've worked all the way around the cob.

FENNEL Although its bulb is delicious raw or cooked, fennel's feathery fronds give the most flavor raw, so many recipes call for separating the bulb from the fronds. If you picture a fennel bulb as a hand, cut the tops off where the rings would be on its "fingers." The bulb's core softens when you cook it, but remove it if you're using fennel raw.

GREENS Many dark, leafy greens, such as kale, chard, or collards, have a tough rib running down their middle. Unless you'll be braising the greens (cooking them in liquid for a long period of time), remove the rib. The easiest way: Fold each leaf in half lengthwise, and run a knife down both sides of the rib simultaneously to cut it out.

HERBS Fresh herbs can be divided into two general categories. Soft herbs, such as parsley, chives, basil, chervil, tarragon, dill, and cilantro, have edible stems and are best added to recipes fresh. They can be torn and added to salads in big pieces, or chopped finely for more widespread flavor. Woody herbs, such as rosemary, thyme, oregano, marjoram, mint, and sage, are usually picked off their stems before chopping and are often cooked, rather than added fresh. To strip leaves off woody herbs, hold the herb sprig by its top with one hand, and pull the leaves off by running the thumb and index finger of your other hand down the length of the stem. All herbs are finely chopped when the board you're chopping them on begins to turn green.

MANGOES We know they're delicious, but how to cut them? You can peel perfectly ripe mangoes with a good vegetable peeler, then cut the flesh off the pit. The important part is knowing which direction to cut. If you imagine the mango as a flat football, hold it like it's ready to be kicked, and cut each flat side off, leaving a 1-inch section in the center where the pit is, then slice the flesh. If the mango isn't quite ripe, cut the sides off with the skin intact, score the flesh in a checkerboard pattern, and push each half inside out, so the squares pop out—then chew or cut the fruit off the skin.

SQUASH Cutting through a squash can take quite a bit of exertion. It's necessary if you're going to serve it in slices, but if it's soft, mashable squash or pumpkin you want, you can skip the work. Start with a big variety, such as kabocha, and roast it—whole—at 400°F, until soft when poked with a skewer. Let it cool, cut it open, scoop the seeds out, and then use the flesh.

FROM *the* SHOPS

RECIPE LIST

THE GIRLS' GUIDE TO PICKING AND CHOOSING:
How to Shop at Sur La Table on a Budget

It's nice to walk into Sur La Table with a mission. With its expansive cookware displays and beckoning rows of gadgets, the Pike Place Market's biggest kitchen store is an easy place to lose oneself. Today, all I want is a spoonula. I should be in and out in five minutes.

A spoonula is a cook's most versatile utensil. It's built like a plastic rubber spatula, with a business end that withstands heat well, but it's spoon shaped, allowing the wielder to both scrape into the rounded corners of any pan and carefully taste what's cooking. Small spoonulas are perfect for exploring the depths of a mustard jar; big ones stir braises exactly like a traditional wooden spoon, but better. Yet somehow—until today—I've survived without one. If I had a million dollars, I might shop here more, but I don't tend to be that impulsive when it comes to kitchen equipment, because I know there's always a way to improvise. But spoonulas. Spoonulas are affordable.

When I open Sur La Table's Pine Street door, I'm distracted by a giant display of Le Creuset. There, on the bottom shelf, hidden under the rows and rows of colorful casseroles, is the tagine I've been flirting with for years (when my All-Clad isn't looking). It's an attractive flame-red color, and it will allow me to make that Berbere Chickpea and Carrot Tagine (page 93) taste much more authentic than it does cooked in my normal stainless-steel pan—the dish *is*

named for the pot itself, after all. And at $175, it's practically a bargain, especially considering I'll probably use it at least three times each year. (And soon, I'll have the perfect tool for stirring those tagines.) I hoist it onto my hip and head for the utensils, feeling smug and a little more Moroccan.

But wait, what are *these*? Olive pit dishes! How adorable. They're small and simple, and they come in gorgeous shades of yellow, green, and red, with PITS stamped into the ceramic on the side, so that when you put them next to a bowl full of olives, people know what they're for. (How clever!) And wait . . . oh my God, could it be? The red version is almost the same red as the tagine that's now perched precariously between one arm and my purse. You know, sometimes

when you cook Moroccan food, there are olives involved. I don't know about you, but when I get a chance to raid the olive counter for a recipe, I always go a little overboard, and I invariably have olives left over. These little bowls are the perfect solution—and since I usually only cook North African food when we have company, I always need a little munchie out for our guests. Hello! Olives. I'll get two, just in case, and I'll sell that useless little Orrefors crystal bowl on Craigslist to pay for them. My hips swing a little, because the tagine is starting to get heavy. My five minutes are up; I'm just going to make a quick spin through the gadgets on my way to the spatula section.

Hey, wow. I didn't know you could buy square canning jars with those old-fashioned flip lids. I mean, I love how everyone's into canning these days, and I don't mean to complain about receiving great blackberry jam or tomato sauce, but isn't it annoying how all the jars are exactly the same? I mean, just the other day, I walked all the way down to the basement to grab a jar of ginger apricot sauce and came up with peach jam without realizing it. I should get some of these little square numbers for next summer's preserving, so that I can differentiate between everything I make. Yes, I'll put all my vegetable pickles in square jars. But I'll only get the small and medium sizes; that big size is just too expensive. (I'm happy to give up a week's worth of lattes but going without for a month would be overkill.) I open five or six of them, poke a finger through the loop end of each top, and dangle them from the fingers on the hand that's not holding the tagine with the olive bowls inside.

On to the cooking utensils. I wonder whether it's better to buy a spoonula with a wooden handle or a metal handle. I prefer the look of the wooden handle, but the metal ones are dishwasher-safe, which is a big bonus. I'll get one of each, and look, here's a spatula with little pigs on it! How darling. My son will totally love it. Mission accomplished.

Except I'm not sure how to pick the utensils up. Three of my fingers are turning blue, and my purse, which is half-supporting $200 worth of ceramics, is starting to slide off my shoulder. I look behind me; no one's watching. I press the tagine hip against the spatula display, thinking I'll scoot the pot onto the shelf for just a second and grab what I need. Only, the tagine's top starts sliding off, so I have to lunge forward, pressing the top between my chest and the shelf to keep it from crashing to the floor. Now I'm basically grinding against the utensils display, my canning jar hand twisted awkwardly out behind me.

"May I offer you a basket?" asks a small voice. The people here are always so kind. The saleswoman starts by rescuing the glass—looking out for the welfare of other customers is always a good first step—and then gently extracts me from the rest of my predicament. (What a friend.) Finally, we've stacked all of my belongings-to-be, including the spoonulas, into the basket. She volunteers to take it to the counter. "I love this tagine," she gushes as we pass an Italian-themed display on our way to the front. "It's funny, but I find it a great way to keep cooked pasta dishes warm too."

Pasta! I wanted to cook pasta for dinner. I'll grab some of that bucatini and the sauce they have here, so I don't have to make a second trip to the store. (Gas is so expensive these days.) And that large-grain Israeli couscous, doesn't it look so pretty in a glass jar like that? It's really the only thing to serve under a tagine. Into the basket it goes.

My eyes scan the register area as the saleswoman rings everything up. I pass on the vintage Italian olive oil dish towels—I think I have everything I need for now, and I just can't justify another dish towel. (Stingy Swiss genes.) I'm perfectly chuffed at my decision making until a large three-digit number flashes before my eyes. I take a deep nasal breath. I pinch my lips together. The number is $46.07 more than my absolute upper spending limit for the day. Sheepishly, I reach for the three spoonulas, which add up to about that amount. "Actually, I think I'll grab these next time," I tell my new friend, setting them aside to indicate I won't be taking them home. "Sure!" she chimes. Phew. She understands. I mean, everyone has to heat their house, and I have half a dozen perfectly good wooden spoons at home.

Sur La Table's Pike Place Market store has everything you could possibly need for your kitchen—and possibly a few things you just want. It's a cook's paradise.

CHOCOLATE CHUNK BANANA COFFEE CAKE
with PIKE PLACE ROAST STREUSEL

This moist, sweet treat has a mouthful of a name, which is appropriate, because once this comes out of the oven, you'll spend a bit of time unable to speak. Its coffee flavor, which lurks in the background behind hunks of gooey chocolate, comes from ground Starbucks Pike Place Roast coffee beans, rather than the espresso powder typically used in baking. The blend was released in 2008 to celebrate the Market's place in Starbucks's history.

Whole wheat flour gives this coffee cake an earthier flavor, but you can use only all-purpose flour (1½ cups total) if you prefer. In a pinch, use another coffee with bold flavors and a smooth finish.

active time **35 minutes** | *makes* **one 10-inch cake**

for the streusel

¼ cup (packed) light brown sugar
1 tablespoon finely ground Pike Place Roast coffee beans
¼ cup walnuts, finely chopped

for the coffee cake

Baking spray, or butter and flour, for the pan
¾ cup all-purpose flour
¾ cup white or regular whole wheat flour
¾ teaspoon baking powder
½ teaspoon baking soda
¾ teaspoon kosher salt
2 tablespoons finely ground Pike Place Roast coffee beans
¾ cup (1½ sticks) unsalted butter, softened
½ cup (packed) light brown sugar
½ cup sugar
2 large eggs
1 tablespoon vanilla extract

- First, make the streusel: Mix the streusel ingredients together in a small bowl and set aside.

- Preheat the oven to 350°F. Prepare a 10-inch tube pan with baking spray (or grease with butter and dust with flour) and set aside.

- Make the coffee cake: Whisk the all-purpose and whole wheat flours, baking powder, baking soda, salt, and coffee beans together in a large bowl. In the work bowl of a stand mixer fitted with the paddle attachment (or using a hand mixer), cream the butter, brown sugar, and sugar together on high speed until light, about 2 minutes. Add the eggs one at a time, mixing until blended between additions and scraping the side of the bowl when necessary. Add the vanilla and stir until blended. Add a third of the dry ingredients and mix on low speed until just combined. Add the mashed banana, then another third of the dry ingredients, then the sour cream, then the remaining dry ingredients, mixing on low speed until just combined each time. Fold in the chocolate by hand. Transfer the batter to the prepared pan, smooth it flat with a spatula, and sprinkle the streusel evenly on top.

1½ cups (about 3 large) mashed ripe
  bananas
½ cup sour cream
8 ounces semisweet chocolate, finely
  chopped

- Bake for 50 to 60 minutes, or until the top is browned and beginning to crack and a skewer inserted into the middle comes out with just a few crumbs attached.

- Cool the cake in the pan for 10 minutes. Run a small knife around the edges, then invert it first onto a cooling rack, then onto a serving plate (right side up). Let the cake cool for another 10 minutes (so the chocolate sets up a little inside), then slice it and serve warm.

PROFILE: *Starbucks Coffee Company*

Named for Captain Ahab's first mate in *Moby-Dick*, to conjure up the days when coffee was a seafarers' trade, Starbucks is now more than forty years old. Its first store opened in the Pike Place Market in 1971, and the rest is history—Starbucks now has more than 17,000 stores in more than fifty countries worldwide. Outside its landmark store in the Market, you'll find tourists tapping along with the gospel quartet often found busking outside or posing under the two-tailed siren on the original sign. (You might notice she's slightly less modest than the one on Starbucks's cups today.)

HONEY CREAM BISCUITS

If you can get past the allure of Moon Valley Organics's honey-scented skin care products at its Pike Place Market day stall, you'll also find delicious honey, harvested in Washington's Cascade Mountains. Use it to make these biscuits, which are perfect for breakfast, served straight from the oven. Spread them with butter and—what else?—a little more honey.

active time **15 minutes** | *makes* **8 biscuits**

3 cups all-purpose flour, plus more for rolling
1 teaspoon kosher salt
1½ tablespoons baking powder
¾ cup (1½ sticks) cold unsalted butter
1 cup plus 1 to 2 tablespoons heavy cream
¼ cup high-quality honey
1 tablespoon melted butter

- Preheat the oven to 425°F. Line a baking sheet with parchment paper and set aside.

- Whisk the flour, salt, and baking powder together in a mixing bowl. Cut the cold butter into ½-inch chunks, and using a large fork or a pastry cutter, mix the butter into the flour until the butter resembles small peas. Add 1 cup of the cream and the honey, drizzling the honey evenly over the entire mixture, and mix with a fork until no dry spots remain.

- Knead the dough a few times in the bowl to help it hold together (you may need to add another tablespoon or 2 of cream), then turn it out onto a very lightly floured counter. Roll it into a roughly 8-inch circle (about ½ inch thick), then use a 3-inch biscuit cutter or a drinking glass to cut out round biscuits, rerolling the last bit of dough for more biscuits.

- Invert the biscuits onto the prepared baking sheet, so the smooth side is up (they'll rise up, but not out), brush with the melted butter, and bake for 12 to 15 minutes, until puffed and golden brown. Let cool 5 minutes on the sheets, then serve warm.

GARLICKY GOAT CHEESE MOUSSE

If you haven't been there before, finding Maximilien, the little French restaurant at the back of the Pike Place Market (looking out over Puget Sound), can be tough. Wind your way behind Pike Place Fish, between Don and Joe's Meats and MarketSpice, and you'll be rewarded with sweeping views and killer happy hour deals in the bar upstairs. Besides great *frites*, traditional *moules marinières* (mussels in white wine sauce), and a French-inspired take on chicken wings, you'll find an earthy, pungent goat cheese and garlic spread—just make sure everyone at your table gets a toast smeared with it.

You can make this version up to three days ahead. Cover whatever bowl(s) you use with plastic wrap, chill, and bring the mousse to room temperature before serving.

active time **20 minutes** | *makes* **enough appetizer spread for 8**

---

3 large cloves garlic, smashed
¼ teaspoon whole dill seed
1½ teaspoons chopped fresh thyme
1 green onion, chopped
Kosher salt and freshly ground black pepper
1 (11-ounce) log goat cheese, softened
1½ tablespoons heavy cream

■ In a food processor, pulse the garlic, dill seed, thyme, green onion, and salt and pepper to taste until very finely chopped, scraping down the sides of the bowl between pulses if necessary. Add the goat cheese and heavy cream, and whirl to blend. Season to taste with additional salt and pepper, if necessary. (Alternatively, finely chop the ingredients and mash them together in a medium bowl with a large fork.) Transfer to a serving dish just big enough to hold the spread (or use several small bowls) and serve.

DEVILED DUCK EGGS *with* GREEN OLIVES, SMOKED PAPRIKA, *and* FRIED CAPERS

On the north side of the two-way glass cases that enclose Pike Place Market Creamery, the Market's little dairy emporium, there's an egg case that beats any grocery store by a mile. In addition to chicken eggs in all sizes, plus quail, goose, and even decorative ostrich eggs, you'll find big, rich duck eggs. For supersize appetizers, use them for these deviled eggs. This Spanish-inspired version, studded with green olives and topped with crisp fried capers, is a showstopper.

Since duck eggs can vary in size, consider adding a bit more or less mayonnaise, depending on how big the yolks are. To make this with regular eggs, substitute eight extra-large eggs for the duck eggs.

active time **30 minutes** | *makes* **12 deviled egg halves**

6 duck eggs
3 to 4 tablespoons mayonnaise
2 teaspoons Dijon mustard
½ teaspoon *pimentón de la Vera* (smoked Spanish paprika; see page 75 for where to purchase)
Kosher salt and freshly ground black pepper
¼ cup finely chopped green olives
Olive oil, for frying the capers
2 tablespoons capers

- Place the eggs in a medium saucepan, add cold water to cover, and bring to a boil over high heat. As soon as water boils, remove the pan from the heat, cover, and let sit 15 minutes (13 minutes for extra-large eggs).

- Drain the eggs and cool them in a pan of ice-cold water for 15 minutes.

- When the eggs are cool, peel and halve them lengthwise. Transfer the yolks to the work bowl of a stand mixer fitted with the paddle attachment and the whites to a serving plate. To the yolks add the mayonnaise, mustard, *pimentón*, and salt and pepper to taste, and whip until they are smooth and fluffy. (You can also use a fork to blend the ingredients together in a medium bowl.) Fold in the olives, and spoon or pipe the yolk mixture into the egg whites.

- Heat about ¾ inch of olive oil in a small saucepan to 325°F (measured with a deep-fat thermometer), or until the oil shimmers. Pat the capers dry on paper towels, then fry them for 3 to 4 minutes, or until the capers have opened and the frying bubbles are very small. Use a small strainer or slotted spoon to transfer the capers to a paper towel to drain, then garnish the eggs with them. Serve immediately.

NOTE: If you don't have a piping bag but want your deviled eggs to look a little fancy, scoop the filling into a large zip-top bag. Cut a ½-inch triangle off one bottom corner and squeeze the filling out of the hole, into the egg whites.

SPICY MARINATED FETA

There is nothing soft-spoken about the products at Sotto Voce, the infused oil and vinegar boutique in the Pike Place Market's Triangle Building. Though its classic *olio santo*, a robust oil infused with herbs, garlic, and spices, is most popular, I love the heat of the company's Olio Buon Gustaio, which is all you need to fire up a package of pasta. Here, the latter is drizzled over a slab of feta (you could also use a goat cheese, such as *bûcheron*), along with sun-dried tomatoes and oregano. Serve the appetizers with toasts that can soak up the oil.

For this recipe, I use bulk feta, like the kind the folks at DeLaurenti's cheese counter slice fresh. If you're using a regular block of feta from a grocery store cheese section (usually a 7-ounce block), use the entire thing.

active time **10 minutes** | *makes* **4 servings**

¼ pound feta cheese
2 cloves garlic, finely chopped
Pinch of crushed red pepper flakes
1 teaspoon chopped fresh oregano
1 tablespoon chopped, oil-packed
    sun-dried tomatoes
¼ cup chili and garlic olive oil, such as
    Sotto Voce's Olio Buon Gustaio
Sea salt and freshly ground black
    pepper

■ Place the feta in a wide, rimmed bowl. Sprinkle the garlic, red pepper flakes, oregano, and sun-dried tomatoes over the top, drizzle with the oil, then season to taste with salt and pepper. Let sit at room temperature for 1 hour, then serve with toasts.

NOTE: The feta can be assembled up to a day ahead, without the salt and pepper, then brought to room temperature and seasoned 1 hour before serving.

MEXICAN-SPICED SOPAIPILLAS

Walk into the Pike Place Market's Mexican Grocery and you might drown in decision anxiety. Do you head straight to the counter to order a tamale, or paw through the spices? Do you reach out to crinkle the dried chilies, because you know you have to touch them even though it's clear you probably shouldn't, or do you stock up on house-made tortillas? I vote for all of the above. And when you get home, make sopaipillas.

Traditionally, sopaipillas can be either sweet or savory. In many South American countries, they are fried, sauced, and served as a main course. The Mexican (and often New Mexican) dessert version is made by frying fresh flour tortillas until they puff and blister, then dousing them with cinnamon and sugar. Here's a new take: fry, then dust your chips with a mixture of spices, sugar, and salt, for a sweet and spicy treat any time of day.

active time **20 minutes** | *makes* **4 servings**

Canola oil, for frying
6 (6-inch) flour tortillas
1 tablespoon plus 1 teaspoon sugar
2 teaspoons kosher salt
1 teaspoon ancho or chipotle chile
    powder
½ teaspoon ground cinnamon
2 teaspoons ground cumin

- Heat ½ inch canola oil to 350°F (measured with a deep-fat thermometer) in a large, deep skillet over medium-high heat. While the oil heats, cut each tortilla into 6 wedges and mix the sugar, salt, chile powder, cinnamon, and cumin together in a small bowl.

- Add a small piece of tortilla to the oil; if it sizzles vigorously, the oil is hot enough. Carefully add about 10 of the tortilla wedges to the oil. Fry for 20 to 30 seconds on each side, or until both sides are puffed and golden brown. Transfer to a paper towel–lined plate and season *immediately* with the spice mixture on one side. Repeat with the remaining tortillas and spices, and serve warm.

NOTE: Instead of making this spice mixture, you could use the Chili Spice from Alex's Vegetable Chili (page 69), sweetened with a bit of sugar and seasoned with salt.

MARKET TIP: *Buying Spices*

Spices aren't usually kept in the refrigerator, but they do go stale; buy spices as close to the day you'll use them as possible.

BERBERE CHICKPEA *and* CARROT TAGINE

At World Spice Merchants, just outside the Market's technical boundaries, there are tissue boxes everywhere. "If you're not sneezing, you're not in a spice shop," its employees are fond of saying. And sneeze you will! Lined with rows and rows of freshly ground spices and house-made curries, seasoning rubs, herb blends, and teas, World Spice is a scratch-and-sniff extravaganza for grown-ups, where what you need is ground to order. Plan to spend a few extra minutes perusing its cookbook library.

Made with World Spice's Berbere blend, which contains cloves, fenugreek, ginger, cardamom, cassia, Telli-cherry pepper, coriander, pequin chiles, and rare ajowan seeds, this sweet and spicy tagine is based on the simple Moroccan stew named for the cone-topped clay pot it's typically cooked in. It's a great example of how an intensely flavorful spice mixture can invigorate a simple weeknight supper. Order the blend online (see Resources, on page 193) or substitute a basic curry powder.

If you'd like, cool and garnish the tagine with a scoop of creamy Minted Yogurt Dipping Sauce (page 68).

NOTE: You may omit the raisins, but they dissolve to give the dish a wonderful sweetness.

---

active time **25 minutes** | *makes* **4 servings**

1 tablespoon unsalted butter
1 tablespoon canola oil
1 medium yellow onion, chopped
2 cloves garlic, finely chopped
Kosher salt
1 to 2 tablespoons World Spice
    Merchants Berbere spice blend
2 large tomatoes, chopped, or 1
    (15-ounce) can diced tomatoes
4 cups (two 15-ounce cans) cooked
    chickpeas, drained and rinsed if
    using canned
1 cup vegetable or chicken broth
¼ cup golden raisins
3 large carrots, peeled and cut into
    ½-inch rounds
3 tablespoons chopped fresh cilantro
    or parsley
Israeli (or regular) couscous, cooked,
    for serving

- Heat a large skillet with a lid over medium heat. When hot, add the butter and oil. When the butter has melted, add the onion, and sauté until it is soft, about 5 minutes. Add the garlic, season to taste with salt, and add the Berbere spice. Cook, stirring, until the spices are fragrant, about 1 minute.

- Add the tomatoes, chickpeas, broth, raisins, and carrots, stir to combine, and bring to a simmer. Reduce heat to the lowest setting, cover, and cook for 10 minutes. Stir the stew and cook for another 10 minutes, until almost all the liquid has evaporated. Stir in the cilantro and serve immediately, over couscous.

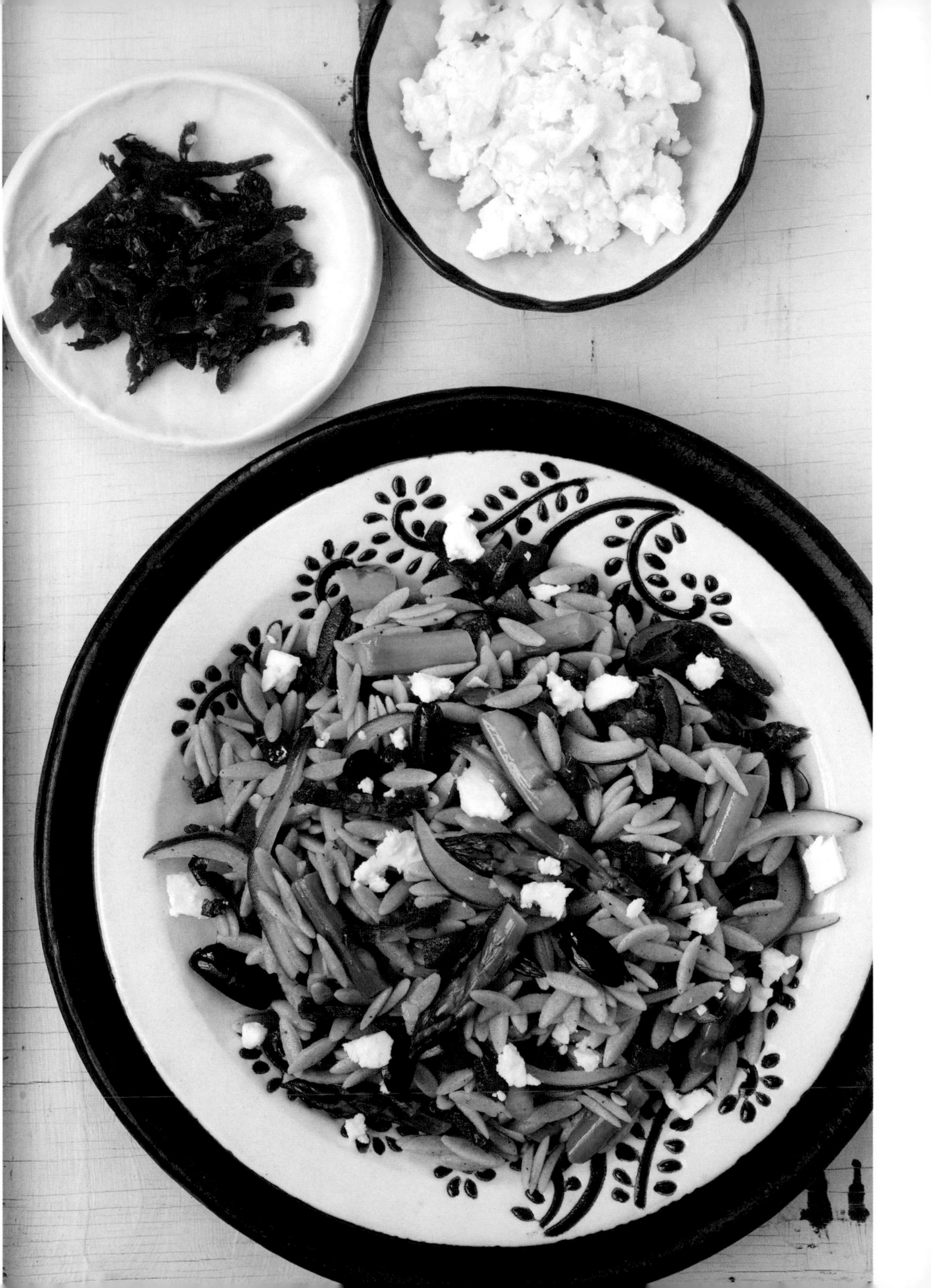

MEDITERRANEAN PASTA SALAD
with SEVEN-GRAIN ORZO

recipe by **Pappardelle's Pasta**

Walk through the halls of the Market's Main Arcade, and you might see folks munching on long, thin strands of something crunchy. It's the chocolate linguine from Pappardelle's, the dried-pasta company that makes pasta in literally every flavor. This springy salad, made with one of the company's tamer varieties, is delicious hot but also makes a great picnic side dish.

To rehydrate sun-dried tomatoes, place them in a small bowl. Add boiling water to cover and let them sit, turning them occasionally, for three to four hours, until they are soft.

active time **30 minutes** | *makes* **6 servings**

4 teaspoons extra-virgin olive oil, divided
2 large cloves garlic, finely chopped
1 small red onion, quartered and sliced
1½ cups (about 2 ounces) sun-dried tomatoes (not oil-packed), rehydrated and thinly sliced
½ pound asparagus, cut into 1-inch pieces
3 tablespoons balsamic vinegar
1 pound seven-grain orzo, such as Pappardelle's
1 red bell pepper, stemmed, seeded, and diced
1 cup chopped kalamata olives
¼ pound (about 1 cup) crumbled feta cheese
Kosher salt and freshly ground black pepper

- Bring a large pot of water to a boil for the pasta.

- Heat a large skillet over medium-high heat. Add 2 teaspoons of the oil, then the garlic, onion, sun-dried tomatoes, and asparagus. Sauté for 3 to 5 minutes, or until the onion begins to soften. Add the vinegar and cook another minute or so, or until the vinegar glazes the pan. Set aside and allow to cool to room temperature.

- Meanwhile, cook the pasta until al dente, 8 to 10 minutes. Drain and immediately toss with the remaining 2 teaspoons olive oil. Add the vegetable mixture, along with the bell pepper, olives, and feta, and season to taste with salt and pepper. Serve hot or at room temperature.

ORECCHIETTE PASTA *with* CAULIFLOWER CREAM *and* SHAVED BLACK TRUFFLES

recipe by **Anthony Polizzi, of Steelhead Diner**

Although La Buona Tavola carries all sorts of Italian products, it's perhaps best known for its imported black truffles, which the employees coddle with the utmost care. It's no secret that these little suckers are pricey—which means if you're going to splurge on them, you should shower paper-thin slices over a dish that puts them on a culinary pedestal. This rich pasta, which Steelhead Diner serves in the fall, is perfect. The servings aren't huge, but there's nothing light about it—serve a big green salad (like the Salade Verte on page 58) afterward.

It's best to use a good vegetable peeler (or even better, a mandolin) to shave the truffle into paper-thin slices, because you'll get the most flavor that way. If you don't want to invest in a black truffle, simply make the pasta without it. Drizzle the final product with truffle oil or sprinkle liberally with truffle-infused sea salt.

active time **45 minutes** | *makes* **4 servings**

1 head (about 2 pounds) cauliflower
2 tablespoons olive oil, divided
¼ cup finely chopped onion
4 cloves garlic, chopped, divided
2 cups heavy cream
1 bay leaf
Kosher salt
2 cups orecchiette
1 small shallot, finely chopped
½ cup dry sherry
1 small (about 1 ounce) black truffle
1 tablespoon unsalted butter
¼ teaspoon crushed red pepper flakes
1 tablespoon finely chopped fresh
    parsley
1 cup baby spinach
Parmesan cheese, for garnish

- Bring a large pot of water to a boil for the cauliflower. Meanwhile, core the cauliflower and cut it into bite-size pieces. When the water boils, add about two-thirds of the florets, setting the rest aside for later, and cook for 3 minutes, until almost tender. (It will cook more later.) Use a slotted spoon to transfer the cauliflower to a large bowl, and set aside. Keep the water hot, as you'll also be cooking the pasta in it.

- Next, heat 1 tablespoon of the olive oil in a large skillet over medium heat. Add the onion and half the garlic, and cook, stirring, for 5 minutes, or until soft. Add the uncooked cauliflower, cream, bay leaf, and salt to taste, and bring to a bare simmer—do not let the mixture come to a boil. Cook, stirring occasionally, until the cauliflower is tender, about 5 minutes more. Remove the bay leaf, then carefully puree the mixture in a blender or food processor. Set the cauliflower cream aside.

- Bring the water back to a boil, then cook the orecchiette al dente according to package instructions. Drain and set aside.

- Wipe the skillet out and heat it again, this time over medium-high heat, and add the remaining tablespoon oil. Add the reserved cauliflower and cook for 3 minutes, undisturbed, or until the florets are browned on one side. Stir the cauliflower, add the remaining garlic and the shallot, and cook for 1 or 2 minutes more, until the garlic is toasted. Add the sherry, and cook for 3 minutes, or until the alcohol has cooked off completely. Add 2 cups of the cauliflower cream and 6 slices of black truffle, and bring to a simmer. Add the butter, red pepper flakes, parsley, and spinach, and cook, stirring, for a minute or 2, until the spinach wilts. Add the cooked pasta and simmer for another minute, or until the pasta has soaked up some of the sauce. Serve immediately, garnished with Parmesan and thin black truffle shavings.

HOT-SWEET MANGO PICKLES

Wandering into Oriental Mart can be a little, well, disorienting. Packed with stacks of ingredients from China, Japan, Thailand, and Vietnam (just to start), it's a cross between a mini-mart and a full-scale Asian grocery—only the staff are endlessly helpful, and the kitchenette in the back has a whole menu worth exploring. Ask them where to find the rice vinegar and fish sauce you'll need for this recipe.

These pickles make an excellent snack, sandwich partner, or salad topping—but note that they will get spicier the longer you leave them in the brine. For tips on slicing mangoes, see page 78.

active time **15 minutes** | *makes* **4 servings**

2 large, almost-ripe mangoes, peeled, pitted, and sliced into ½-inch spears
1 cup rice vinegar
½ teaspoon kosher salt
2 teaspoons sugar
Pinch of crushed red pepper flakes
2 cloves garlic, finely chopped
1 tablespoon finely chopped fresh cilantro
½ teaspoon fish sauce, such as nuoc cham or nam pla

- Combine all the ingredients in a bowl just big enough to hold all the mangoes. Let sit at room temperature for about 15 minutes for the flavors to blend, stirring occasionally, then serve.

ZA'ATAR-CRUSTED CHICKEN
with HARISSA-YOGURT SAUCE

Although walking into The Souk, on the north end of the Pike Place Market, may be intimidating for those unfamiliar with Indian, Middle Eastern, and North African foods, it's actually a haven for ingredients that make quick, creative dinners. On its shelves you'll find *za'atar*, a dried herb and spice mixture often made with thyme, oregano, savory, dried sumac, salt, and sesame seeds—you may find it lends itself well to other dishes you make regularly, like roasted potatoes. You'll also find harissa, a North African chili sauce, which lends gentle heat to the ultra-simple yogurt sauce that accompanies the chicken here. (Both *za'atar* and harissa are available at The Souk.) For a dinner filled with new flavors, serve this dish with Berbere Chickpea and Carrot Tagine (page 93); together, they'll serve 6 people.

active time **15 minutes** | *makes* **4 servings** | *equipment* **Kitchen string, for tying the chicken legs**

1 (5-pound) whole chicken, patted dry
   with paper towels
2 teaspoons olive oil
1 teaspoon kosher salt
2 tablespoons *za'atar*
¾ cup plain yogurt
2 to 3 teaspoons harissa

- Preheat the oven to 425°F.

- Rub all parts of the chicken with the oil. Place the bird on a roasting rack set over a roasting pan. Combine the salt and *za'atar* in a small bowl, then sprinkle the entire chicken with the spice mixture. Fold the wings behind the chicken's back, tie the legs together with kitchen string, and sprinkle any remaining spice on any bare spots.

- Roast the chicken for about 1 hour, or until the breast meat measures 165°F on an instant-read thermometer. If the skin is dark golden brown before the meat is done, slide a baking sheet onto an oven rack above the chicken.

- Meanwhile, stir the yogurt and harissa together in a small bowl and let sit at room temperature while the chicken roasts.

- When the chicken is done, let it rest for 10 minutes, then carve and serve hot, with the yogurt sauce.

MARKET TIP: *Preparing a Chicken for Roasting*

Here's the most useful thing I learned in culinary school: preparing a chicken for roasting means channeling a day at the beach. To roast a bird, imagine yourself settling in for a day of sunbathing. First, you lie down. You raise your arms high above your head, then tuck your hands behind your head, elbows out, and close your eyes toward the sun. Now, do this to your chicken—wings tucked back, breast up—and it's ready for its roast.

GETTING TECHNICAL: *Cheese-Making at Beecher's Handmade Cheese*

If you walk by the corner of Pike Place and Pine Street on a sunny day, you'll see throngs of cheese lovers peering into the windows of Beecher's Handmade Cheese, where fresh batches of award-winning cheddars, jacks, and curds are made every day. Under the guidance of head cheesemaker Brad Sinko, Beecher's most popular product, its Flagship Cheddar, looks easy enough to make. Workers clad head to toe in white suits mill around, stirring huge open vats of milk or cutting curds into smaller pieces. But get behind the windows, and you'll learn there's a lot more chemistry involved.

The first load of farm-fresh milk arrives at Beecher's before dawn each morning. Coming from cows fed according to the company's exacting specifications, the milk is pumped at about 90°F into the large stainless-steel tank visitors see from the outside. To begin, the milk is pasteurized, then inoculated in the "make vat" with a starter culture, which contains bacteria that consume the lactose in the milk, producing the lactic acid that helps give cheddar cheese its hallmark flavor and texture.

After about forty-five minutes, the mixture is coagulated with rennet, an enzyme that causes milk to separate into curds, which are solid, and whey, which is liquid. After another thirty-five minutes, when the milk has gained the texture of thick pudding, the cheesemakers cut it into pea-size cubes. They start cooking the curds extremely slowly, raising the temperature by only two degrees every ten minutes, until the mixture reaches 101°F. (This is when the starter culture is most active.) For the next forty-five minutes, the cheese is stirred vigorously, to prevent the curds from knitting together.

Next, the curds and whey are pumped onto a drain table, where the whey drains out and the curds stack together to form a large bed, and the "cheddaring" process begins: the bed of curd is cut into ten-pound loaves, which are then flipped and stacked for two hours, to allow more whey to drain out. Scientifically, the fats and proteins in the cheese line up in parallel as it sits, giving cheddar its traditional firmness. During this time, Sinko and his team assess the cheese's acid levels. When the slabs reach a certain acidity, they're chopped into small curds, then salted (this stops the acid growth), and shoveled (literally!) into forty-pound cheese moulds. The moulds are pressed overnight, to remove yet more whey, then the cheese is wrapped and cut for the eighteen-month storage process it undergoes before hitting store shelves.

DeLAURENTI
ITALY — TUSCANY
IL FORTETO
PECORINO "BIGIO"
SOTTOCENERE
SHEEP   38.99 LB

USA — SANDGATE, VERMONT
NORTHERN SPY FARM
GOAT SONG TOMME
RM
GOAT $43.99 LB

USA —
O
Ho
GOAT

10 WAYS ► *with Cheese*

GRILLED GINGER- *and* MASCARPONE-STUFFED FRENCH TOAST
Slice challah bread into 1-inch-thick slabs, then cut each slice almost all the way in half again, leaving the flat bottom end of the bread intact. Spread the sides gently and spread one of the inner halves with ginger jam and the other with mascarpone cheese. Soak the bread in a mixture of eggs, vanilla extract, half-and-half, and ground ginger, and grill (or cook on a griddle) over medium-low heat.

CHERRY–GOAT CHEESE BRUSCHETTA
Mix halved, pitted cherries with shredded basil, olive oil, balsamic vinegar, and salt and pepper to taste. Spoon onto baguette slices smeared with soft, fresh goat cheese.

PEPPER JACK CHIPS
Sprinkle ½ pound grated pepper jack cheese (such as Beecher's Marco Polo or a jalapeño jack) evenly across a parchment-lined baking sheet. Bake for 10 to 12 minutes in a preheated 425°F oven, until caramel colored. Cool until firm, then break into chips.

CAMEMBERT *with* HONEYED WALNUTS
Blend ½ cup chopped walnuts with 2 tablespoons warm honey. Spoon onto a room-temperature wedge of camembert or brie and serve with sliced apples or thin toasts.

ASPARAGUS, MINT, *and* RICOTTA SALAD
Drizzle roasted asparagus with great olive oil and freshly squeezed lemon juice, then top with finely chopped mint and a shower of fresh, crumbled ricotta.

WARM QUINOA, SQUASH, WHITE BEAN, *and* PARMESAN SALAD
Cook ¼ cup red quinoa in ½ cup plus 1 tablespoon water with 1 cup chopped butternut squash. Stir in half a can of white beans and some chopped herbs, then drizzle with olive oil and top with

a flurry of freshly grated Parmesan. This makes an excellent lunch for one.

GREEK CUCUMBER *and* FETA BITES
Top skin-on cucumber slices with rounds of sliced roma tomatoes, then a baby salad of chopped olives and crumbled feta cheese seasoned with salt, pepper, chopped onions, olive oil, and red wine vinegar.

PASTA *with* GREENS *and* GOAT CHEESE
Make the Three Greens Tart with Goat Cheese and Pine Nuts (page 66), only instead of baking the ingredients on puff pastry, mix them with hot pasta.

BLUE CHEESE SHORTBREAD
Omit the lavender, vanilla extract, and ¼ cup of the butter from the Lavender Shortbread (page 146), and replace the butter with 4 ounces of softened blue cheese. Bake as directed and serve as part of a cheese platter for dessert.

WATERMELON *and* BURRATA CHEESE SALAD
For dessert, arrange chopped, firm seedless watermelon next to a scoop of fresh burrata. Drizzle with honey and sprinkle with chopped mint before serving.

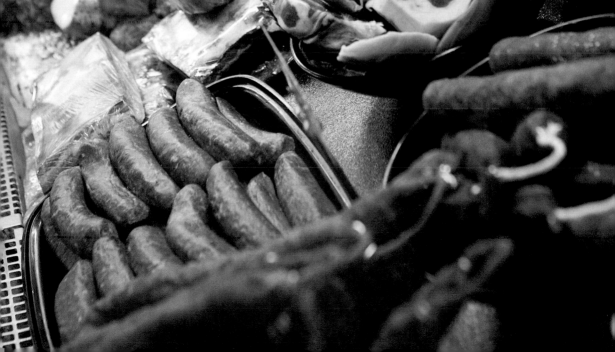

FROM *the* BUTCHER

RECIPE LIST

TO MARKET, TO MARKET:
Following a Pig Through the Pike Place Market

The Pike Place Market may be world renowned for fish, but its heart belongs to a pig. In February 2011 a runaway taxi hit Rachel, the life-size brass oinker that banks donations to the Market Foundation. During her brief absence for repairs, Seattle mourned. Not only does Rachel the Pig stand sentry for photographs in front of Pike Place Fish, but she also serves as a city mascot; she's the always-smiling Market hostess who dependably welcomes regular visitors and tourists alike. Once she was rehabilitated, we gave her a heroine's welcome home: she beamed from the bed of the Market's green pickup truck as she made her way through town like a prom queen.

It may not just be coincidence that, from an eater's perspective, the Pike Place Market is also home to a palate-pleasing variety of porcine products. From Uli's Famous Sausage's bratwurst to Bavarian Meats's bacon to DeLaurenti's cured meats, the Market is a porkmonger's paradise. And despite serious space restrictions, many purveyors make their own charcuterie and break down their own animals right at the Market—like making jam or pickles or fresh cheese, it's a practice that's resurged not just because it's hip, but because it's also both economical and delicious.

Nowhere does the pig get more respectable treatment than at Matt's in the Market, the restaurant opened by Matt Janke in the Corner Market Building in 1996. Near a window that overlooks Rachel the Pig, I joined chef Chester "Chet" Gerl to see just how a chef turns a fresh pig into some of the Market's most famous fare.

Admittedly, it seems a little sardonic to stand at Chet's butcher table in early winter, preparing to slice into a 106-pound animal while likenesses of Rachel trot across the Market's roof across the street, eight-tiny-reindeer style. (They're called the "swinedeer.") But as soon as he starts talking about making a stock rich with anise, rosemary, thyme, and coriander, my stomach speaks louder than my conscience.

I've never seen a pig being butchered before, and as Chet walks me through it, rather than thinking about carving up an animal, I find myself naming its body parts in terms of what dishes they'll create. After he takes off the trotters (the feet), which he'll use for head cheese, Chet takes off the shoulder, which he'll rub with cumin and coriander, braise, and serve in posole, a deeply spiced Mexican stew made with chilies and hominy. Then he slices away the belly. Since this pig is relatively large, its belly will get cooked and preserved in its own fat as confit, then sliced for Vietnamese-style *banh mi* sandwiches, but the bellies of smaller animals are used to make *porchetta* or sausage. Chet is working quickly; clearly, it takes him more time to explain to me what he'll do with the pig's meat than it would if he were just carving—and it must be called carving, not cutting or hacking; the man makes no unnecessary movement, and every extra edible sliver of meat is whittled away from the bone and set aside for stock or pâté. Next, he shows me the tiny hanger steak and the tenderloin along the pig's backbone before he moves toward its hindquarters. That afternoon, the back legs will be braised in a rich mixture of chilies and charred onions, then slathered in a coffee-rich sauce—a quintessentially Seattle twist on the barbecued pulled-pork sandwich (see Pulled-Pork Sandwiches with Stumptown Barbecue Sauce on page 120), which has helped make Matt's one of Seattle's most popular lunch spots.

As Chet cuts into the animal's torso, the sun sets over Puget Sound, and cold December air whips in over the beast's back, bringing with it the scent of the evergreens for sale on the street below. We're up on the third floor, so we can see all the Christmas lights glittering; this must be the best view in the Market.

I'm a little shocked when Chet starts hacking into the ribs and cuts off the pig's head in one fell swoop; I'm realizing that what was once clearly an animal is now, nineteen minutes later, just piles of meat in various plastic tubs. A very small part of me considers vegetarianism, until Chet cleans up and brings me a slice of the pork belly pâté he stuffs with pistachios, spikes with cognac, and bakes wrapped in bacon. Topped with sweet fennel pickles, it's a charcuterie lover's fantasy. I savor every bite and hope out loud that every customer does the same.

GERMAN SPLIT PEA SOUP

recipe by **Bavarian Meats**

Walking up to the counter at Bavarian Meats can be a bit intimidating–understandable, when the place is packed with a selection of cured meats most Americans aren't familiar with and a crowd ordering knockwurst and *land-jäger* in German. Never fear; the ladies behind the counter are unfailingly helpful and cheerful. In fact, I'd recommend walking in without a recipe, because listening to their instructions is always a pleasure. Declaring that every household needs a soup, Gabrielle Kessler described this split pea soup recipe to me while I shopped, noting how it gets a gentle smoky flavor from the smoked ham hock. You can also make the same soup with lentils, in which case you should season it right at the end with a dollop of German mustard and a swig of good vinegar.

NOTE: According to Gabrielle, sweet onions aren't appropriate here. Look for the kind with firm brown skin.

active time **45 minutes** | *makes* **6 servings**

2 tablespoons olive oil
1 medium yellow onion, thinly sliced
1 large carrot, peeled and chopped
1 rib celery, chopped
2 large cloves garlic, smashed
Kosher salt and freshly ground black
    pepper
1 (1½-pound) smoked ham hock
4 cups Homemade Chicken Stock
    (page 185) or store-bought chicken
    broth
2 cups water
2 bay leaves
¾ teaspoon dried dill
½ teaspoon ground cardamom
1 pound dried split peas

- Heat a large, heavy soup pot over medium heat. When hot, add the oil, then the onion, and cook, stirring occasionally, for about 10 minutes, or until the onion is soft. Add the carrots, celery, and garlic, season to taste with salt and pepper, and cook another 5 minutes, stirring occasionally. Add the ham hock, stock, water, bay leaves, dill, cardamom, and split peas, stir, and bring to a simmer. Reduce the heat to low and cook at a bare simmer until the peas are soft and the meat falls off the bone, about 1½ to 2 hours. Remove the bay leaves.

- Transfer the ham to a cutting board and set aside. Carefully puree the soup in small batches in a blender or food processor (or using an immersion blender), and return it to the pan. Add additional water, if necessary, to thin the soup to your desired consistency, and rewarm it over low heat. Finely chop the meat, discarding the bones and any fatty parts, and add it back to the soup. Check seasonings (you probably won't need much salt because the meat is usually salty enough) and serve hot.

SMOKY BACON *and* KALE GRATIN

Seattle celebrity chef Tom Douglas has always championed Bavarian Meats, the Pike Place Market's German sausage mecca. Specializing in wursts, wieners, cold cuts, and all things Bavarian for more than 50 years, the family-run business is also famous in Seattle for its bacon, which is cut to order and carries a hearty, smoky flavor. While she's slicing, ask Uta Adamczyk, one of the meat mavens behind the counter, for something new to try. She never leads me astray.

To prepare the kale for this warming side dish, chop the tough ends off right where the leaves begin to sprout from the stalk. Gather the kale leaves together in groups and cut them into ¼-inch strips across the stalk, almost like cutting basil into chiffonade (long, thin ribbons). Once the kale is cut, it's easier to soak and spin dry in a salad spinner. Also, feel free to use any type of kale.

active time **30 minutes** | *makes* **4 to 6 servings**

3 thick strips smoky bacon, cut into ¼-inch dice

1 bunch (about 1¼ pounds) lacinato kale, cut into ribbons (about 6 packed cups chopped), rinsed, and dried

Kosher salt and freshly ground black pepper

1 cup Homemade Chicken Stock (page 185) or store-bought chicken broth

2 tablespoons all-purpose flour

1 tablespoon butter, cut into tiny cubes, plus more for buttering the dish

¼ cup grated Parmesan cheese

½ cup heavy cream

- Preheat the oven to 375°F.

- Heat a large, deep skillet or soup pot over medium heat. When hot, add the bacon, and cook for about 10 minutes, or until almost crisp. Add the kale, season to taste with salt and pepper, and cook for 5 minutes, stirring, or until the kale turns bright green. Add the stock, cover the pot, and cook for 10 minutes, stirring once or twice. Take the lid off the pot and cook the kale for another 5 minutes or so, until no liquid remains at the bottom of the pot. (You want the kale to be fairly dry.)

- Remove the pot from the heat, add the flour, and stir until no white remains. Butter a medium oval gratin dish (a pie plate or several small crème brûlée dishes or large ramekins will work as well) and add the kale in a roughly even layer. Check the kale for seasonings, dot with the butter, and sprinkle the Parmesan evenly over the top. Drizzle the cream over the cheese, and bake for 30 minutes, or until the cream is bubbling and the cheese is browned. Serve warm.

SPANISH CHICKPEA *and* CHORIZO STEW

Made with chorizo from Uli's Famous Sausage, in the Market's Main Arcade, this easy stew has hints of Spain. Some chorizos are spicier than others; pick one that matches your hankering for heat.

active time **40 minutes** | *makes* **4 servings**

1 pound (about 4 links) chorizo, such as Uli's Famous Sausage's, casings removed
1 tablespoon extra-virgin olive oil
1 medium onion, chopped
2 cloves garlic, finely chopped
2 large carrots, peeled and cut into ½-inch-thick half moons
½ cup dry white wine
Kosher salt and freshly ground black pepper
½ teaspoon *pimentón de la Vera* (smoked Spanish paprika; see page 75 for where to purchase)
2 teaspoons tomato paste
1 (15-ounce) can chickpeas, rinsed and drained
4 cups Homemade Chicken Stock (page 185) or store-bought chicken broth
1 tablespoon sherry vinegar
2 tablespoons chopped parsley (optional)

- Heat a large, heavy-bottomed soup pot over medium heat. When hot, crumble the chorizo into the pan and cook, stirring once or twice, until browned through, about 6 to 8 minutes. Break the sausage up into small bite-size pieces, then transfer it to a paper towel–lined plate to drain. Set aside.

- Add the olive oil to the pan, then the onion. Sauté for about 5 minutes, or until the onion begins to soften. Add the garlic and carrots, stir, then add the wine and bring it to a simmer, using a wooden spoon to scrape the brown bits off the bottom of the pan. Simmer until no liquid remains, stirring occasionally.

- Season the vegetables to taste with salt and pepper, then stir in the *pimentón* and tomato paste. Add the chickpeas, stock, and reserved chorizo, and bring to a simmer. Cook the stew for about 20 minutes, stirring occasionally. Stir in the vinegar and parsley, season to taste, and serve hot.

NOTE: This stew can be made 2 to 3 days ahead and reheated before serving.

PROFILE: *Uli Lengenberg, of Uli's Famous Sausage*

Sporting giant black work boots, professorial spectacles, his characteristic handlebar moustache, and a sweatshirt bearing his own likeness, German master butcher Uli Lengenberg is a Pike Place Market icon. In 1999 Uli (pronounced "OOH-lee") opened his little sausage shop, making everything from bratwurst to *boudin blanc* for shoppers to buy fresh or enjoy grilled (with a beer, naturally). Uli concedes that not all people can cook from their heart, without consulting a recipe, so he's always willing to suggest what to do with, say, D'Avignon or Merguez sausage. Then he'll volunteer to show you how to eat it.

GREEK CHICKEN SALAD

Demetrios Moraitis, the owner of Mr. D's Greek Delicacies, is perhaps most famously known among Market savants for his "yeero" sculptures, made with frozen gyro meat. Although you won't find his artwork–busts of people like the Clintons, Mona Lisa, or Socrates–on display at the deli, you will find delicious gyros, spanakopita, and Greek salads. His Greek chicken salad consists of lettuce topped with kalamata olives, tomatoes, cucumbers, thick tzatziki sauce, and skewered grilled chicken, fragrant with garlic and oregano. In this version, the yogurt sauce binds a chopped chicken salad that relies on all the same flavors. Pile it into pita bread with a bit of arugula, eat it plain, or hey–make a sculpture. It's your salad.

active time **35 minutes** | *makes* **4 to 6 servings**

for the **chicken**

2 tablespoons olive oil
2 cloves garlic, finely chopped
1 tablespoon chopped fresh oregano
¼ teaspoon crushed red pepper flakes
1¼ pounds boneless, skinless chicken
   breasts, trimmed

for the **tzatziki sauce**

1 scant cup (one 7-ounce container)
   plain whole Greek yogurt
2 cloves garlic, finely chopped
¼ cup mayonnaise or Homemade
   Aioli (page 184)
¼ cup finely chopped fresh parsley
Kosher salt and freshly ground black
   pepper

for **assembly**

2 tomatoes, diced, or ½ pint grape
   tomatoes, halved
1 small cucumber, peeled (if desired)
   and diced
½ cup kalamata olives, pitted and
   chopped
4 ounces (about 1 cup) crumbled feta
   cheese

- First, marinate the chicken: Combine the olive oil, garlic, oregano, and red pepper flakes in a medium bowl. Add the chicken, turn to coat, and refrigerate, covered, for at least 1 hour or up to 24 hours.

- Meanwhile, make the tzatziki sauce: Combine the yogurt, garlic, mayonnaise, and parsley in a small bowl. Season to taste with salt and pepper, and set aside, refrigerating if necessary.

- Prepare a grill for direct cooking over medium-high heat, about 400°F to 450°F. When the grill is hot, brush the cooking grates clean, then transfer the chicken to a plate, leaving the extra oil behind. Season the chicken to taste on both sides with salt and pepper. Grill the chicken, smooth side down first, covered, for 5 to 7 minutes, or until the chicken releases easily from the grates. Turn and grill another 3 to 5 minutes, or until the meat is firm to the touch and cooked through. Transfer the chicken to a plate and let cool for 10 minutes.

- To assemble the salad, chop the chicken, transfer it to a large bowl, and gently combine it with the tomatoes, cucumber, olives, and feta, along with as much of the tzatziki sauce as you'd like. Serve immediately or chill and serve cold.

NOTE: If you plan to make the salad ahead, let the chicken cool thoroughly before you cut it up, so the residual heat doesn't cook the tomatoes and cucumbers.

MALT-ROASTED CORNED BEEF REUBEN

recipe by **Gary Marx, of The Pike Pub**

The Pike Place Market happens to be home to an astounding number of great sandwiches. Consider the Reuben: Three Girls Bakery, known for its granola and rugelach, has a back sandwich counter that's been operating since 1912; it makes a simple-but-sensational version served on house-made seeded rye bread. I Love New York Deli serves the classic stacked sammy to go. But if you have time for a sandwich and a beer, hit The Pike Pub. Its Reuben—made with beef first braised in beer, then roasted with the malt syrup sometimes used in beer brewing until it's shellacked with a glossy sheen—is earthy and sweet. For a taste of the real thing, make these Reubens with Apple Sauerkraut (page 168) instead of regular store-bought sauerkraut.

Market Cellar Winery, located on Western Avenue, sells the golden malt syrup used here. You won't need the entire container for this recipe; use the remainder in place of honey when you make granola or in a traditional Jewish honey cake.

NOTE: Since the meat requires chilling time, start this recipe in the morning or let the meat chill overnight before continuing.

---

active time **1 hour 15 minutes** | *makes* **4 big sandwiches**

for the **beef**

1 (2½-pound) raw corned beef brisket
2 cups Pike Brewing Company's
   Tandem Double Ale or similar dark
   Belgian-style ale
1 cup water
½ cup golden malt syrup

for the **russian dressing**

1 cup mayonnaise
1 tablespoon Worcestershire sauce
¼ cup ketchup
¾ teaspoon prepared horseradish
1 tablespoon freshly squeezed lemon
   juice

■ First, braise the beef: Preheat the oven to 350°F. Place the beef in a roasting pan, fat side up, and add the beer and water. Cover with a lid (or seal well with aluminum foil) and braise for 3 hours. Carefully pour off the liquid and scrape about half the fat off the top of the meat. Pour the malt syrup directly over the top of the meat, increase the oven temperature to 400°F, and roast, uncovered, for 15 minutes more, basting the beef with the pan juices halfway through cooking. When the top is dark and glazed, remove the beef from the oven and let stand at room temperature for 30 minutes. Refrigerate (in its liquid, if possible) until firm, at least 3 hours.

2 tablespoons finely chopped onion

2 tablespoons finely chopped green bell pepper

Kosher salt and freshly ground black pepper

for **assembly**

8 slices good rye bread

1½ tablespoons unsalted butter

½ pound sliced emmentaler cheese

¼ pound prepared sauerkraut, warmed

Half-sour pickles, for serving

- Meanwhile, make the russian dressing: Place the mayonnaise, Worcestershire sauce, ketchup, horseradish, lemon juice, onion, and bell pepper in a blender or food processor, and puree until smooth. Season to taste with salt and pepper, then transfer to a bowl and refrigerate until ready to use.

- To assemble the sandwiches, slice the meat as thinly as possible against the grain. Place in an aluminum foil–covered casserole dish and gently reheat for 10 minutes at 350°F, if necessary.

- While the meat reheats, spread each slice of bread with a thin layer of the butter. Heat a large skillet over medium-low heat. Place two of the bread slices in the pan, buttered sides down. Top one with a slice of emmentaler and spread the other with russian dressing. When the bread is toasted and the cheese has melted, transfer the cheesy toast to a plate. Heap with corned beef and sauerkraut, then top with the russian-dressed toast. Slice in half and serve immediately, with a pickle spear. Repeat with the remaining ingredients.

- If you prefer to serve all the sandwiches at once, place all the bread buttered side down on a baking sheet and toast in the oven (with cheese and dressing) while the meat warms.

VIETNAMESE CURRIED CHICKEN
and SQUASH STEW

recipe by **Thoa Nguyen, of Thoa's Restaurant & Lounge**

When it comes to Vietnamese cuisine, *ca ri ga* may not have the star power of *pho* or spring rolls, but it's deeply warming and easy to make on a weeknight–just marinate the chicken before you leave for the day. This version, from Thoa's, the Vietnamese restaurant on Union Street (one block south of the Pike Place Market), is made with kabocha squash and boneless, skinless chicken thighs. Serve it over steamed rice or hot rice vermicelli noodles, so you can enjoy every last drop of the creamy coconut curry.

Yes, you can eat the skin on a kabocha squash–it steams into an almost silky texture. Use an orange-skinned one if the green kind makes you uneasy. I use an ice cream scoop to take the seeds out.

active time **30 minutes** | *makes* **4 to 6 servings**

3 tablespoons curry powder (such as Three Golden Bells brand), divided

½ teaspoon kosher salt

2 pounds boneless, skinless chicken thighs, trimmed and quartered

2 tablespoons canola or peanut oil

1 small shallot, finely chopped

2 teaspoons finely chopped garlic

1 to 2 teaspoons ground chile paste (such as Thai Kitchen brand yellow curry paste) or crushed red pepper flakes

¼ cup fish sauce, such as nuoc cham or nam pla

1 tablespoon sugar

2 cups Homemade Chicken Stock (page 185) or store-bought chicken broth

2 stalks lemongrass, cut into 3-inch pieces

1 (2-pound) kabocha squash, halved, seeded, and cut into 1-inch cubes

- Mix 2 tablespoons of the curry powder and the salt together in a small bowl. Place the chicken pieces on a plate and sprinkle them evenly with the curry mixture on both sides. Cover the chicken with plastic wrap and refrigerate for at least 30 minutes.

- Heat the oil in a large, ovenproof heavy-bottomed pot with a tight-fitting lid (such as a Dutch oven) over medium heat. When the oil is hot, add the shallots, garlic, chile paste, and the remaining 1 tablespoon curry powder, and stir until fragrant, about 10 seconds. Add the chicken and cook until the edges of the pieces are golden, about 4 to 5 minutes per side. Add the fish sauce, sugar, and chicken stock. (The stock won't quite cover everything.) Bruise each piece of the lemongrass with the flat side of a large knife, like you're crushing garlic, and add to the pot. Bring to a simmer, add the squash, and cook, covered, over low heat for 15 minutes.

1 (14-ounce) can coconut milk
1 small yellow onion, cut into wedges
Chopped fresh cilantro or Thai basil,
    for garnish
Steamed rice or rice noodles, for serving

- Remove the lid and stir in the coconut milk and the onion. Bring the stew back to a simmer, replace the lid, and cook, covered, over low heat until all the vegetables are tender, another 15 to 20 minutes. Transfer the stew to a serving bowl and garnish with basil or cilantro. Serve immediately, over rice.

DOWNTOWN DUCK SALAD

recipe by **Brian Jones, of Pear Delicatessen & Shoppe**

Pike Place Market's Pear Delicatessen & Shoppe is known for its fantastic beer selection and its creative sandwiches. The best is the Downtown Duck, which features pulled five-spice-roasted duck piled high on a toasted brioche bun with Asian slaw and *sriracha* aioli. Here, owners Lisa Martin and Brian Jones have deconstructed the sandwich, turning it into a make-ahead luncheon salad with a mango-ginger vinaigrette you'll want to drink straight. If you like a little crunch, top the salad with Homemade Croutons (page 154) made with brioche.

Don and Joe's Meats carries fresh duck, but if you can't find it, plan ahead. Many stores only sell frozen duck, and a small duck takes 2 or 3 days to thaw in the refrigerator.

active time **1 hour 15 minutes** | *makes* **6 servings**

for the **duck**

1 (5-pound) duck, rinsed and patted dry
3 tablespoons Chinese five-spice powder
2 teaspoons kosher salt
1 teaspoon freshly ground black pepper
¼ cup hoisin sauce

for the **mango-ginger vinaigrette**

½ cup packed, drained pickled ginger (from one 6-ounce jar)
1 (16-ounce) bottle mango juice drink, such as Odwalla's Mango Tango
1 tablespoon Dijon mustard
2 tablespoons rice vinegar
1 tablespoon toasted sesame oil
½ cup extra-virgin olive oil
½ to 2 teaspoons *sriracha*

- First, roast the duck: Preheat the oven to 350°F. Trim the fat flap off the duck's neck and cut off the tail end below the thighs. Cut the wings off at the middle joint. Prick the skin with a paring knife, making about 20 incisions (through the skin only) over the breast and legs of the bird.

- In a small bowl, combine the five-spice powder, salt, and pepper. Using your hands, rub the spice mixture all over the duck, inside and out. Transfer the duck to a roasting pan fitted with a roasting rack and roast for 75 to 90 minutes, or until the legs pull loosely away from the body and the inside measures 165°F with an instant-read thermometer. Set the duck aside to cool for at least an hour.

- While the duck cools, make the vinaigrette: In a blender or food processor, whirl the ginger, mango drink, mustard, rice vinegar, and sesame oil until smooth. With the machine running, add the olive oil in a slow, steady stream, and process until the oil is completely integrated. Season to taste with the *sriracha*, then transfer the dressing to a container and set aside.

for the **Asian slaw and salad**

1 (1¼-pound) napa cabbage, sliced into ¼-inch strips

1 small red bell pepper, stemmed, seeded, and thinly sliced

1 small yellow bell pepper, stemmed, seeded, and thinly sliced

1 cup loosely packed chopped fresh cilantro

4 medium carrots, peeled and grated

1 cup chopped green onions, green parts only (reserve the white parts for another use)

6 ounces mixed salad greens

- Prepare the Asian slaw: In a large bowl, toss the cabbage, red and yellow bell peppers, cilantro, carrots, and green onions to blend. Refrigerate until ready to serve.

- When the duck has cooled, remove its skin and discard. Using your hands or two forks, pick the meat off the duck's breast, legs, and thighs, and shred it into small pieces. Transfer the duck to a large mixing bowl and stir in the hoisin sauce and about ¼ cup of the vinaigrette. Refrigerate until ready to serve.

- To serve, toss the Asian slaw with vinaigrette to taste. Divide the greens among 6 plates and drizzle them with a bit of extra vinaigrette, then top with equal portions of slaw and pulled duck.

PULLED-PORK SANDWICHES
with STUMPTOWN BARBECUE SAUCE

from **Chester "Chet" Gerl, of Matt's in the Market**

At Matt's in the Market, the bustling, bright little restaurant that looks out over the Pike Place Market's main entrance, chef Chet Gerl breaks down whole pigs on a giant butchering table. The shoulders always go to making the rich, coffee-spiked pulled-pork barbecue sandwich that regulars come back for again and again. The sauce has a bit of kick, so mix some of it in with the pork and save some for slathering on the buns (you can use any type of bun, but I think brioche is best), so that those who like spice can add more. Combined with the crunch of a chipotle-spiked red cabbage slaw, it's the ultimate pulled-pork sandwich—unless, of course, you've already finished it.

Since the braised pork needs to cool in its liquid before you shred the meat, it's best to start this recipe either early in the morning or the day before you want to serve it. And the larger the pork shoulder you use, the more people this will serve—there's plenty of sauce.

active time **90 minutes** | *makes* **8 sandwiches**

for the **braised pork**

1 (3- to 4-pound) pork shoulder, strings left intact if applicable
Kosher salt and freshly ground black pepper
2 tablespoons vegetable oil
1 large sweet onion, chopped
3 cloves garlic, smashed
2 dried ancho chiles, stems broken off
2 bay leaves
½ cup roughly chopped fresh oregano
1 cup San Marzano tomatoes (from a 15-ounce can), crushed

for the **barbecue sauce**

1 dried ancho chile
1 large sweet onion, peeled and quartered
6 cloves garlic, peeled

continued

- First, braise the pork: Preheat the oven to 300°F. Heat a large, ovenproof heavy-bottomed pot with a tight-fitting lid (such as a Dutch oven) over medium heat. Season the pork to taste on all sides with salt and pepper. When the pot is hot, add the oil, then the pork, and cook, turning occasionally, until seared caramel brown on all sides, 25 to 30 minutes total. Add the onion, garlic, and chiles, and cook for 5 minutes more, stirring occasionally. Add the bay leaves, oregano, and tomatoes, plus enough water to almost completely cover the pork (about 6 cups), and bring to a simmer. Cover the pot and transfer it to the oven. Cook for 2½ hours, turning the pork halfway through, or until the meat pulls apart easily. Set the pork aside at room temperature to cool in its liquid, covered.

- While the pork is cooling, make the sauce: Place the ancho chile in a small bowl and add boiling water to cover. Set aside. Preheat the broiler to its highest setting. Place the onion, garlic, tomatoes, and tomatillos on an unlined baking sheet and broil, 2 or 3 inches from the heating unit, turning them occasionally, until the vegetables are charred on all sides. (You may have to remove the vegetables at different times.) Set aside to cool.

2 small beefsteak tomatoes

4 tomatillos, husked

2 tablespoons canola oil

2 tablespoons fresh high-quality
    ground coffee, such as Stumptown

2 chipotle peppers in adobo sauce

½ cup freshly squeezed orange juice

2 cups ketchup

2 tablespoons honey

¼ cup apple cider vinegar

2 tablespoons tequila

Kosher salt and freshly ground black
    pepper

for the **slaw**

2 cups finely shredded red cabbage
    (from about ½ small cabbage)

½ cup fresh whole cilantro leaves

1 tablespoon freshly squeezed lime
    juice

2 tablespoons mayonnaise

1 small chipotle pepper in adobo
    sauce, very finely chopped

8 brioche buns, toasted

- Heat a large saucepan over medium heat. When the pan is hot, add the canola oil, then the reserved vegetables, ground coffee, and chipotles; sauté until soft, about 10 minutes. Drain the ancho chile; stem, seed, and chop it; and add it to the pan along with the orange juice and ketchup. Turn the heat to low and simmer the sauce for 15 minutes, then stir in the honey, vinegar, and tequila. Puree the sauce in batches in a blender or food processor until completely smooth. Season to taste with salt and pepper, plus additional vinegar, honey, or adobo sauce from the chipotles, as desired. Return the sauce to the pot and keep warm (if serving the sandwiches within 2 hours), or refrigerate and reheat over low heat for 20 minutes, stirring occasionally, until thoroughly warmed, before mixing with the pork.

- An hour or two before serving, make the slaw: Combine the cabbage, cilantro, lime juice, and mayonnaise in a large bowl, adding the chopped chipotle to taste.

- When the pork has cooled, remove it from the liquid, discarding the liquid. (You can also strain the liquid, refrigerate it overnight, skim off any fat, and use it as stock for soup.) Using your fingers or two forks, pull the pork into shards, making sure to get rid of as much fat as possible.

- Blend the meat with about ¾ of the hot barbecue sauce, reserving the remaining sauce for spreading on the buns.

- To serve, spread sauce to taste on the bottom halves of the buns. Top with pulled pork and slaw, then the top buns. Serve immediately.

NOTE: The pork can be shredded and mixed with sauce up to 2 days ahead. To reheat, place it in a casserole dish, cover with aluminum foil, and heat in a 300°F oven for 15 to 20 minutes, until heated through.

BRAISED HANGING TENDER *with* WILD MUSHROOMS, ROSEMARY, *and* JUNIPER

When I asked Don Kuzaro Jr. of Don and Joe's Meats for two pounds of hanging tender, he looked at me suspiciously. "You the butcher's daughter?" he asked. He was only half kidding—traditionally, butchers saved it for themselves, because the cut (also called hanger steak or onglet) contains a tough central membrane that is removed before cooking. As the name implies, it's meltingly tender when braised. Made with juniper, smoky bacon, and rosemary, this dish is no exception—the resulting sauce tastes like it's been braised with the scent of a Pacific Northwest forest. Serve the beef, sauce, and mushrooms over something that soaks up flavor well, such as polenta, Israeli couscous, or egg noodles.

Call a good butcher ahead and ask about trimming, if you don't feel comfortable doing it yourself; the guys at Don and Joe's are always helpful. And if you'd like, use flank steak instead; it works beautifully.

active time **90 minutes** | *makes* **4 servings**

for the **beef braise**

2 thick strips smoky bacon, diced

2 pounds hanging tender, cut into 4 to 6 pieces, membrane removed

Kosher salt and freshly ground black pepper

1 large onion, chopped

1 large carrot, peeled and chopped

2 cloves garlic, smashed

½ pound cremini mushrooms, rinsed, trimmed, and sliced

1 tablespoon tomato paste

6 black peppercorns

8 juniper berries

3 (6-inch) sprigs fresh rosemary

4 (3-inch) sprigs fresh thyme

2 tablespoons porcini powder, optional

1 cup dry red wine

continued

- Preheat the oven to 325°F.

- First, braise the beef. Heat a large, heavy-bottomed pot with a tight-fitting lid over medium heat. When hot, add the bacon and cook, stirring occasionally, for 5 minutes, or until the bacon grease coats the bottom of the pot. (If there isn't enough grease, you can add 1 tablespoon canola oil.) Scoot the bacon to the edges. Season the beef to taste with salt and pepper, and add it to the pot. Brown the pieces of beef on all sides, turning occasionally, 15 to 20 minutes. (You may need to work in batches.) Transfer the beef pieces to a paper towel-lined plate and set aside.

- Add the onion, carrot, garlic, and mushrooms to the pan with the bacon, season to taste with salt and pepper, and cook, stirring occasionally, until the onion begins to soften, about 10 minutes. Add the tomato paste, peppercorns, juniper berries, rosemary and thyme sprigs, and porcini powder, and stir until the tomato paste is evenly distributed. Add the wine, bring to a simmer, and cook for 2 minutes, using a wooden spoon to scrape any brown bits off the bottom of the pan. Add the stock, return the beef pieces to the pan, and bring the mixture to a bare simmer. Cover the pan and transfer it to the oven. Braise the beef for about 2 hours, turning the pieces once about halfway through, or until the meat comes away easily in shreds when you pull at it with a fork.

2 cups veal stock, Homemade Chicken Stock (page 185), or store-bought chicken broth

1 tablespoon unsalted butter

for the mushrooms

2 thick strips smoky bacon, diced

1 tablespoon unsalted butter

1 pound assorted wild or cultivated mushrooms, rinsed, trimmed, and quartered

Kosher salt and freshly ground black pepper

2 teaspoons chopped fresh thyme

1 teaspoon chopped fresh parsley

Polenta, Israeli couscous, or egg noodles, for serving

■ Transfer the beef to a plate, cover with aluminum foil, and set aside. Strain the braising liquid into a medium bowl through a fine-mesh strainer, pressing on the solids to squeeze every last drop of goodness, then discarding the solids. Set ⅔ cup of the braising liquid aside. In a large saucepan, cook the remaining liquid at a strong simmer for 10 to 20 minutes, until reduced by half.

■ While the sauce reduces, make the mushrooms: Heat a large skillet with a tight-fitting lid over medium heat. When the skillet is hot, add the bacon and cook until crisp. Transfer the bacon with a slotted spoon to drain on a paper towel–lined plate, and set aside. Add the butter to the pan. When it has melted, add the mushrooms, seasoning them to taste with salt and pepper. Stir in the thyme, and cook, covered, for 10 minutes, or until the mushrooms have given up their liquid. Remove the cover and cook until the liquid has evaporated. Add the reserved braising liquid and bring to a simmer. Cook until no liquid remains, about 5 minutes. Stir in the parsley and the reserved bacon.

■ Season the reduced sauce to taste with salt and pepper, then return the meat to the pot, coating each piece in the sauce, and cover to keep warm.

■ The beef, sauce, and mushrooms can sit at room temperature for up to 1 hour. Reheat for a few minutes just before serving.

■ To serve, stir the tablespoon of butter into the sauce. Pile the polenta into 4 bowls, topping each with a piece of beef, a pool of sauce, and a big scoop of mushrooms. Serve hot.

$5.00
(includes tax)
YES
SWEETBREADS
KIDNEYS
RABBIT
CAPON
CORNISH GAME HENS
CHITTERLINGS
Welcome Here
6.98
7.75
5.75
12.98

ROAST LEG OF LAMB
with GARLICKY NETTLE PESTO

Don and Joe's Meats offers a perfect example of what a real, old-fashioned butcher does best. There, when you buy a leg of lamb, they're happy to take the bone out, trim it for you, and tie it up into a neat little roast, bundled with the fat side up, so it bakes to a beautiful, even toasty brown. Serve the lamb a full fifteen minutes after it comes out of the oven, slathered with a pesto made with stinging nettles.

Nettles come by their name honestly. When you buy them, freshly foraged, they certainly smart when touched—but cooking denatures their stinging properties, and whirled up into a rich, garlic-studded pesto, they're anything but dangerous. Be sure to transfer them directly into their cooking pot, without touching them. (There's no need to pick them off their stems.)

At the Market, look for nettles from early spring to early summer. They're often sold in plastic bags; ask your produce purveyor to open the bag so you can see that they're still bright green. (Unlike with other greens, it's not wise to pick limp nettles away from the rest of the bunch!)

active time **60 minutes** | *makes* **6 to 8 servings**

for the lamb

1 (4-pound) boneless leg of lamb, trimmed of excess fat and tied
1 (375-milliliter) bottle dry red wine
5 cloves garlic, finely chopped
3 tablespoons chopped fresh rosemary
2 tablespoons chopped fresh oregano
Freshly ground black pepper
1 tablespoon olive oil
Kosher salt

- First, prepare the lamb. About 2 hours (and up to 6 hours) before roasting, marinate the leg: Place it in a large bowl; add the wine, garlic, rosemary, oregano, and pepper to taste; and turn the meat to coat. Refrigerate, turning once during the marinating.

- While the lamb marinates, make the pesto: Bring a large pot of salted water to a simmer for the nettles. Add the nettles directly from their bag and cook, stirring continuously, for 3 minutes. (This denatures their sting.) Transfer them to a colander to drain. When the nettles are cool enough to handle, wrap them in a clean dish towel and wring out as much moisture as possible, as you would for spinach. You'll end up with about a cup of cooked, squished nettles.

- In a blender or food processor, whirl the garlic, pine nuts, and salt and pepper to taste until finely chopped. Add the nettles, breaking them up as you drop them in, then the lemon juice, and whirl until finely chopped. With the machine running, add the olive oil in a slow, steady stream and process until smooth. Add the Parmesan, pulse briefly, and season to taste with additional salt, pepper, or lemon juice. (The pesto can be made ahead and refrigerated, covered, up to 1 week.)

for the **nettle pesto**

½ pound nettles
4 large cloves garlic, smashed
½ cup toasted pine nuts
½ teaspoon kosher salt
Freshly ground black pepper
1 tablespoon freshly squeezed lemon
 juice
1¼ cups extra-virgin olive oil
⅓ cup grated Parmesan cheese

- About 2 hours before dinner, remove the lamb from the marinade, transfer it to a large cutting board, and pat it dry with paper towels. Coat the roast with 1 tablespoon of olive oil, season to taste with salt and pepper, and transfer it to a large roasting pan. Let the lamb stand at room temperature for about 30 minutes.

- Preheat the oven to 400°F and place a rack in the bottom third of the oven.

- About 1½ hours before dinner, put the lamb in the oven. Roast for 60 to 75 minutes, or until the top is deeply browned and the lamb measures 125°F in the center with an instant-read thermometer (for medium-rare; timing will depend on your oven and the shape and thickness of the lamb leg). If the top begins to get too brown before the roast is done, lightly cover the lamb with a piece of aluminum foil or slide a large baking sheet onto the oven rack above. When the lamb has finished cooking, remove it from the oven and let it rest for 15 minutes before carving it into thick slices. Serve immediately with the pesto in a bowl so each person can scoop some onto their lamb.

HOW DO I COOK THIS BEAST? *A Beef Primer for Beginners*

As a general rule, there are two major methods for cooking meats—moist-heat cooking, where the meat is wholly or partially submerged in a liquid and cooked for an extended period of time over low heat, and dry-heat cooking, where the meat is cooked quickly over high heat, and there is no (or very little) liquid involved.

When beef is butchered, the animal is typically divided into cuts that have more connective tissue, which is the tough, sinewy tissue that makes improperly cooked meat impossible to chew, and lean cuts, which are usually more tender. Not to be confused with the white fat, or marbling, that runs through beef, the connective tissue often has a slightly silvery hue.

The animal uses larger muscles more to walk and run, which makes the meat fibers from these big muscles tougher in general. Cooking big, tough cuts (which normally have more connective tissue) slowly, in liquid, typically by braising or stewing, allows the connective tissue to break down, which eventually makes the meat very tender. Any cut identified as a "pot roast," as well as cuts like short ribs, brisket, and beef shank, should be cooked slowly to achieve maximum tenderness.

Cuts from the center of the cow—rib and loin meats, often labeled "steak"—are much leaner than those from the cow's shoulders and hindquarters. Less connective tissue means lean cuts can be cooked more quickly, using dry-heat cooking methods such as grilling, pan searing, stir-frying, broiling, or roasting. However, less natural fat in these cuts means that the meat is more likely to dry out if you overcook it.

Of course, there are a few magical cuts that fall between these two categories and are tender enough to cook quickly over very high heat but rich enough to braise well also. Flank and skirt steaks, as well as the hanging tender (also known as hanger steak), fall into this category.

Still have questions? Ask your butcher. He will help you.

10 WAYS ► *with Charcuterie*

CRUMPET BREAKFAST PANINI
Line halved crumpets (such as those from The Crumpet Shop) with gruyère cheese, sliced prosciutto, and scrambled eggs, and grill in a sandwich press.

DUCK CONFIT BENEDICT
Follow the instructions for the Northwest Eggs Benedict (page 6), replacing the smoked salmon with shredded duck confit.

MELON *and* BRESAOLA
Change up the traditional melon and prosciutto appetizer by draping cantaloupe with thinly sliced bresaola, which is made from beef, rather than pork.

CHORIZO BURGERS
Substitute chorizo sausage for about a third of the meat in your favorite hamburger recipe and top with slices of manchego or Spanish blue cheese.

GUANCIALE CARBONARA
Whisk together 2 large eggs, 1 cup grated Parmesan cheese, a good glug of heavy cream, a handful of chopped parsley or basil, and a ½ pound diced, cooked guanciale (cured pork jowl). Add a pound of piping hot, fresh-cooked spaghetti, and toss until the egg sauce is thoroughly warmed.

PASTA E FAGIOLI *with* PANCETTA
Sauté ¾ pound cubed pancetta, and set aside. Sauté 1 chopped onion, 4 peeled and chopped carrots, 4 chopped celery stalks, and 2 minced garlic cloves in olive oil, then add tomato paste and herbs. Add chicken broth to cover, bring to a simmer, then add a can of white beans, a couple handfuls of small pasta, and a dash of Tabasco. Cook until the vegetables are soft, then stir in the pancetta. Serve with grated Parmesan on the side.

CHICKEN LASAGNA *with* PROSCIUTTO

Slip ultrathin layers of prosciutto into your favorite chicken lasagna recipe, right next to the cooked pasta.

HAM-*and*-BUTTER SANDWICHES

Take a cue from the Market's Le Panier and slap fat slices of butter and thinly sliced ham between two baguette halves, for the ultimate picnic lunch.

SPICY KALE GRATIN

Replace the bacon in the Smoky Bacon and Kale Gratin (page 111) with sautéed hot Italian sausage.

PENNE *with* SOPPRESSATA, SUN-DRIED TOMATOES, OLIVES, *and* PESTO

Toss cooked penne pasta with sliced soppressata (Italian cured dry salami), chopped oil-packed sun-dried tomatoes, chopped kalamata olives, and a healthy scoop of basil pesto (or the Garlicky Nettle Pesto on page 126).

FROM *the* OVEN

Country Wheat
$4.25

Country White
$4.25

Rustic
Grain 5.70

Como
Italian 4.50

Pico
Como 3.50

Mille
Grane
$4.30

Walnut
Wheat
$4.30

Organic Potato
$4.30

Pecan Raisin
$6.00

RECIPE LIST

TRAIL OF BREAD CRUMBS:
A Visitor's Tasting Guide to the Pike Place Market

If there's one problem associated with visiting the Pike Place Market, it's this: the human stomach has inevitable limitations. Some people can eat more than others, but almost no one can eat indefinitely, which means that being forced to choose when and how to sample the Market's vast array of specialties can cause more than a little decision anxiety. Just when you form a plan of attack for your day, another mind-blowing baked smell will sneak out from around a corner, grab you by the lapels, and force you to surrender. And when you're deciding among just-baked chocolate croissants, hot, steamed *hum bao* buns, oven-fresh pizza, and piroshky stuffed with spinach, egg, and cheese, no one wants to play favorites.

Luckily, you don't have to tackle the volume issue alone. Savor Seattle, a company Angela Shen founded in 2007, runs excellent behind-the-scenes Market food tours. It's the ideal way to begin tasting your way through the Market, because the tour allows you to sample small amounts of a huge variety of foods in just about two hours—and, OK, because the tour guide rescues you moments before it seems your head will explode trying to decide what to eat first. After the tour, you can continue on your own for the rest of the day.

First—and this should go without saying—eat a modest breakfast. Bread and water or a cup of coffee should suffice, but don't get too hopped up, because your first stop will be the newer Starbucks, on the corner of Pike Street and First Avenue. There, after a chocolate-laced espresso drink and a treat (think baby peanut butter cupcakes), you'll get rigged up with a geeky sound system that allows the tour to proceed without everyone crowding around the guide. The advantage: You don't have to choose between listening and wandering around.

After a bite (or six) at Daily Dozen Doughnut Company, the Economy Market stall that churns out piping-hot cinnamon-sugar mini doughnuts all morning long, you'll get a quick tour of MarketSpice, the Pike Place Market's oldest shop. Try a small cup of its eponymous black tea, teeming with orange, cinnamon, and clove, and learn why, when it was first made at the turn of the twentieth century, some of its ingredients were actually illegal.

Next, stop for smoked salmon at Pike Place Fish, world-famous for its fish-tossing orange-clad fishmongers (see page 3). You'll sample alder smoked, Indian-candied, and jerked salmon, as well as smoked trout. Get your energy up while you're chewing, because you'll have a chance to step behind the counter and catch a keta salmon yourself, if you're the first to volunteer.

After sampling in-season produce at Frank's Quality Produce, the stall Market-area restaurants rely on for exquisite arugula, sample a couple of Pike Place Chowder's award winners. (For its Market Chowder recipe, see page 12.) Step up behind the display at Chukar Cherries, named for a bird found in the Prosser, Washington, area, where Chukar's cherries come from, and you'll sample a cherry-peach salsa and put any preconceptions about what a chocolate-covered cherry should taste like well behind you.

Here's where your day begins to turn toward lunch. (Still hungry? Good.) Savor the velvety texture of the macaroni and cheese at Beecher's Handmade Cheese while you learn about the cheese-making process, then snag a bite of ham-and-cheese piroshky, a traditional Russian dumpling, at Piroshky Piroshky. (Make sure you ask them about their opening day, when someone snuck $1,000 under their front door to help them get off the ground, or the day they delivered to Bill Clinton's hotel.)

At this point, there's a slight chance you might be getting a little full. You must persevere. The tour's last stop is Etta's, the Tom Douglas restaurant famous for its crab cakes (for its recipe for Mini Dungeness Crab Cakes with Green Cocktail Sauce, see page 7). Bid your tour guide adieu and congratulate yourself—you've now scratched the surface.

Coincidentally, the Pike Place Market is also well designed for digesting. From Etta's, cross Western Avenue to Victor Steinbrueck Park, renamed in 1985 to honor the architect's contributions to the Market's restoration. Collapse onto a bench (with a view of the Olympic Mountains, if you've hit upon a nice day) and rest.

OK, that's enough. Onward! Your goal for the afternoon is to taste the necessaries and gather the rest of what you'll need for your carry-on or a satisfying midnight snack.

There's a good chance you may feel sluggish, so head to the original Starbucks store for a pick-me-up. Once revitalized, you'll have the energy to prepare your snack for later. Start by buying a couple of *landjäger*, a few slices of smoked gouda, and a German pretzel at Bavarian Meats. Pick up some chocolate shortbread at Le Panier, the French bakery whose buttery smells have been driving you crazy for the last two hours. They make the most perfect treat before bed, and you never know how hungry you might be at 10 p.m. And don't forget a poppy seed rugelach at Three Girls Bakery, for the morning.

As the afternoon rolls by, you'll need to try a curry beef *hum bao* at Mee Sum Pastry, a slice of pizza at DeLaurenti, and perhaps a baby cheesecake at The Confectional. When you feel like it's time to wind down, pick your poison: go for English tea and crumpets (with butter and honey, naturally) at The Crumpet Shop, or truck up the hill to Le Pichet, where the bar and a cold Lillet cocktail await—as well as a platter of house-made charcuterie. That is, of course, if you're still hungry.

You may have noticed something particular about your day: until now, you haven't actually entered a proper restaurant. Guess there's always tomorrow.

For a complete list of the shops mentioned, see Shops and Quick Stops on page 193.

WHOLE WHEAT CINNAMON PULL-APART BREAD

If there's one pervasive morning smell in the Pike Place Market, it's cinnamon. The Daily Dozen Doughnut Company douses hot miniature fried orbs with cinnamon sugar, to the pure thrill of kids and adults alike. To the right of Pike Place Fish in the Market's Main Arcade, you'll find Pike Place Bakery. From cookies and cakes to Texas-style doughnuts and fritters, nothing about any of its baked goods is small. (It makes a cinnamon pull-apart bread in a tube pan that's at least 6 inches tall.) Down the street, Cinnamon Works makes cinnamon rolls in a huge array of options—whole wheat, gluten-free, with or without nuts, or done sticky bun–style, just to start.

Since it seemed difficult to choose just one, I came up with the ultimate mix of all three—a whole wheat cinnamon pull-apart bread, made by stacking a few dozen tiny cinnamon rolls into each of two loaf pans and coating them with a sweet orange-tinged glaze. Hot out of the oven, you can pull the rolls apart in layers. Go ahead, let people fight over who gets the glazed top rolls or the gooey, caramelized bottom layer—the recipe makes two pans' worth, so you can freeze one and eat the parts you like best a few days later, when there's less competition.

You can let the bread complete both rises at room temperature, instead of using the proofing method described below, but it will take a few hours each time.

active time **1 hour 15 minutes** | *makes* **2 loaves**

for the rolls

2¼ teaspoons (1 packet) active dry yeast
1 cup warm milk
1 large egg plus 1 large egg yolk
2 cups all-purpose flour, divided, plus more for kneading and rolling
2 cups whole wheat pastry flour
½ teaspoon kosher salt
½ cup (packed) light brown sugar
½ teaspoon ground cinnamon
½ cup (1 stick) unsalted butter, cut into tablespoons, at room temperature, divided

continued

- First, start the rolls: Whisk the yeast, milk, egg, and yolk together in a small bowl. Set aside until foamy, about 5 minutes. Bring a large kettle of water to a boil for helping the dough rise.

- In the work bowl of a stand mixer fitted with the paddle attachment (or using a hand mixer), combine 1 cup of the all-purpose flour, all the whole wheat pastry flour, and the salt, brown sugar, and cinnamon. Mix on low until combined. With the machine on low, add the liquid ingredients in a slow, steady stream, and mix until combined. Scatter 6 of the butter pieces (6 tablespoons) over the dough, and mix on medium speed for another minute.

- Switch to the dough hook, and with the machine on medium-low speed, add the remaining cup of all-purpose flour in 3 additions. When the dough cleans the sides of the work bowl (you may have to add another tablespoon or two of flour), increase speed to medium-high and knead for 3 minutes.

for the **filling**

¼ cup (½ stick) unsalted butter, at
    room temperature
1½ teaspoons ground cinnamon
½ cup sugar
½ cup (packed) light brown sugar

for the **butter drizzle**

2 tablespoons sugar
½ teaspoon cinnamon
¼ cup (½ stick) unsalted butter,
    melted (and still hot)

for the **glaze**

½ cup sugar
½ cup orange juice
⅛ teaspoon ground cinnamon

- Generously butter a large bowl with one of the remaining tablespoons of butter. Transfer the dough to the bowl, cover with a dish cloth, and set aside. Create a makeshift proofing oven: Pour about 8 cups of boiling water into the bottom of a roasting pan or casserole dish. Place the roasting pan directly on the floor of the (cold) oven. Place the bowl with the covered dough on the middle rack and let rise with the oven door closed for about 1 hour, or until the dough has doubled in bulk.

- Use the remaining tablespoon of softened butter to generously grease two 8-by-4-inch loaf pans.

- While the dough is rising, make the filling: In a small bowl, mash all the ingredients together with a spoon until the mixture looks like damp sand.

- Roll the dough out on a lightly floured surface with a lightly floured rolling pin into a roughly 11-by-16-inch rectangle (about the size of two pieces of paper side by side). Brush any excess flour away from both sides of the dough. Scatter the butter/sugar filling evenly over the dough, and press it gently into the dough with your hands. Cut the dough in half lengthwise, so you have two 5½-by-16-inch pieces. Roll the dough up lengthwise into two 16-inch logs, squeezing and pinching it as necessary to keep the rolls fairly tight. Cut each log into 1-inch rolls. Starting with the end pieces first, pile one log's worth of baby rolls into each buttered pan, arranging the rolls in two roughly even layers at odd angles.

- Next, make the butter drizzle: Whisk the sugar and cinnamon together in a small bowl, then stir in the melted butter. Drizzle the butter mixture over the rolls, dividing it approximately evenly between each pan.

- Cover the pans again with the dish cloth and let rise in the oven again (with new boiling water) until the dough almost reaches the tops of the pans. (To freeze the dough for later use, cover one or both pans with buttered aluminum foil before the second rise, then wrap in plastic wrap, and freeze for up to 2 months. Thaw at room temperature for 12 hours, then proof and bake as directed, halving the glaze recipe if you're only baking one loaf.)

- Preheat the oven to 350°F.

- Bake the breads for about 35 minutes, or until the tops are brown, the juices are bubbling, and the center rolls feel firm to the touch.

- Just before the breads come out, make the glaze: Bring all the ingredients to a strong simmer over high heat, stirring until the sugar melts. Reduce the heat and simmer on low for 2 minutes.

- Spoon half the glaze over the hot bread right when it comes out of the oven, dividing it evenly between the two pans. Let the bread cool for 5 minutes, then spoon the remaining glaze evenly over the tops. Let the bread cool for 10 more minutes, then slide a butter knife around the edge of the bread. Invert the bread onto a cooling rack, wrap the base in waxed paper, then invert it onto a serving plate (or return it to a clean loaf pan) with the waxed paper underneath. Serve warm.

NOTE: The cooked, cooled bread can be covered and stored at room temperature overnight and pulled apart the next day, but you can also refrigerate it overnight, then slice and toast it.

HONEY-HAZELNUT GRANOLA

Oregon's known for hazelnuts, but in the shadow of Washington's north Cascade Mountains, Holmquist Hazelnut Orchards grows thin-skinned DuChilly hazelnuts, which are slightly sweeter and more oval shaped than the more common round Barcelona variety—and really don't require peeling. At its tiny Pike Place Market day stall, you can stock up on the raw natural hazelnuts and hazelnut oil you'll need for this vanilla-scented granola—but don't miss trying Holmquist's flavored varieties, for snacking.

active time **20 minutes** | *makes* **about 15 loose cups granola**

1 cup high-quality clover honey
½ cup (packed) light brown sugar
1 (3-inch) piece vanilla bean
6½ cups (one 18-ounce container) old-fashioned oats
4 cups whole raw hazelnuts, roughly chopped
1 cup roasted, salted hulled sunflower seeds
2 teaspoons ground cinnamon
1 cup hazelnut oil

- Preheat the oven to 350°F. Line two baking sheets with parchment paper or silicon baking mats and set aside.

- Combine the honey, brown sugar, and the seeds from the vanilla bean in a small saucepan, and cook over medium heat, stirring occasionally, until sugar has dissolved, 5 to 6 minutes.

- Meanwhile, place the oats, hazelnuts, sunflower seeds, cinnamon, and hazelnut oil in a large mixing bowl. Add the honey mixture, and stir to blend. Divide the granola between the two baking sheets, spreading it in an even layer on each sheet, and bake for 30 to 35 minutes, stirring the granola and rotating sheets top to bottom and back to front halfway through. The granola is done when it's uniformly deep golden brown; one pan may be done before the other.

- Let the granola cool to room temperature on the baking sheets. Break apart and store in an airtight container at room temperature for up to 2 weeks.

MARKET TIP: *Using Vanilla Beans*

Real vanilla beans—the 6-inch-long, dark brown, withered things you see crammed into jars in the grocery store—are best purchased fresh, at places like World Spice Merchants. When they're still soft, you can cut them open with a small, sharp knife and scrape the thousands of tiny black seeds inside into liquids you bake with, to infuse them with rich vanilla flavor. To get the seeds out, run the back of your knife along the inside of the bean, like you're curling a ribbon—if the bean isn't flexible enough for this, wrap it in a damp paper towel and microwave it for 30 seconds or so to soften it. Store used beans in your sugar jar, to give the whole jar a little extra flavor.

WARM PANZANELLA SALAD
with BLISTERED TOMATOES, CORN, *and* BASIL

When I go to a good French bakery like Le Panier, my eyes are dependably bigger than my stomach. Invariably, I come out with more than my family can possibly eat that day—which isn't a problem, as long as I make sure the baguette is what stays out on the counter, where it becomes perfect fodder for a summer panzanella. My version of the warm bread salad, which Italians traditionally make with tomatoes, packs as much summer in as possible, in the form of fresh corn, basil leaves, and a basil-flecked vinaigrette. Make the salad a little heartier by adding chopped grilled chicken or crisp bacon crumbles.

If it's warm, grill the tomatoes, bread, and corn outdoors, instead of baking them—aim for a grill temperature between 400° and 450°F.

active time **25 minutes** | *makes* **4 servings**

1 pound grape or cherry tomatoes
¼ cup plus 3 tablespoons extra-virgin olive oil
Kosher salt and freshly ground black pepper
3 corn cobs, husked
1 baguette
1 recipe Basic French Vinaigrette (page 186)
10 large basil leaves, gently torn
¼ pound (about 1 cup) crumbled feta cheese
½ cup (packed) whole basil leaves

- Preheat the oven to 425°F.

- Place the tomatoes in a roasting pan just big enough to fit them all in one layer. Toss them with 3 tablespoons of the olive oil, season to taste with salt and pepper, and roast on the lowest rack of your oven for 10 to 15 minutes, or until the skins are wrinkled and loose. Transfer the tomatoes to a large serving bowl.

- While the tomatoes are roasting, use a small, sharp knife to cut the corn kernels off the cobs (see Produce Primer on page 78 for an easy corn-cutting technique). Transfer the corn to a bowl, toss with 1 tablespoon of the olive oil, season to taste with salt and pepper, and spread onto about a third of an unlined baking sheet.

- Slice the baguette into 1-inch cubes, put the cubes in a large bowl, and drizzle the remaining 3 tablespoons olive oil onto the bread, stirring and tossing it as you drizzle. Transfer the moistened bread cubes to the baking sheet, next to the corn, in one layer. Toast the corn and the bread for about 10 minutes on the upper rack of your oven, or until the bread is light golden brown.

- Meanwhile, in a blender or food processor, whirl the vinaigrette together with the torn basil and set aside.

- Add the toasted bread and corn to the tomato bowl, then add the feta and whole basil leaves. Drizzle with half the vinaigrette, stir gently so the bread soaks up the dressing, and serve immediately, with extra vinaigrette on the side.

PROFILE: *Daily Dozen Doughnut Company*

Daily Dozen Doughnut Company has been a Pike Place Market fixture since 1986. The tiny stall uses a miniature doughnut depositor to drop and fry doughnuts right before customers' eyes—and it's not just the kids who get mesmerized. After showering them with cinnamon or powdered sugar, the doughnut master—typically a thoroughly tattooed and pierced young Seattleite—performs a little magic show, flipping doughnuts through the air and into a paper bag with a satisfying *thwack*. Owner Barbara Elza, who has fallen in love with the community vibe among the Market's microbusiness owners since she took over the shop in 1990, says that more than half of her business actually comes from regular customers, not tourists. Her slogan is "Be a winner, have doughnuts for dinner." I'd agree whole-heartedly, except that each time she passes me a paper bag of piping-hot doughnuts, I realize that part of the magic lies in their temperature. Eating them cold would be a travesty. So don't plan to take any home—dig in immediately. But be careful: they're hot.

MARKETSPICE TEA CAKE

Although MarketSpice carries more than 140 types of tea, from A to . . . well, Y, it's famous for its cinnamon-orange black tea, which comes in its hallmark orange-and-brown box. Naturally sweet and wonderfully aromatic, it makes a great cup–but you don't have to keep it in the bag, so to speak. Longtime manager Nancy DeWitt even uses it to make a clove-spiked cranberry glaze for holiday ham.

Steeping tea bags in the milk used in this simple cake gives the entire thing a sweet, spicy flavor that's enhanced by the glaze, which is also made with the tea. Although it's delicious warm, this cake is really at its best a day or two after it's made.

active time **25 minutes** | *makes* **one 8-inch cake**

for the **cake**

Oil or butter for greasing the pan
1 cup whole milk
2 bags MarketSpice Cinnamon-
    Orange signature tea
Grated zest of 1 large orange (about 3
    tablespoons)
1¾ cups all-purpose flour
2 teaspoons baking powder
¼ teaspoon kosher salt
¼ teaspoon ground cinnamon
2 large eggs
1 cup sugar
1 teaspoon vanilla extract
½ cup (1 stick) unsalted butter,
    melted

for the **glaze**

¼ cup freshly squeezed orange juice
¼ cup sugar
1 bag MarketSpice Cinnamon-Orange
    signature tea

- First, make the cake: Preheat the oven to 350°F and position a rack in the middle of the oven. Grease an 8-inch cake pan with the oil or butter, and set aside.

- In a small saucepan, bring the milk to a bare simmer. Add the tea bags and orange zest, remove the pan from the heat, and set aside to steep for about 5 minutes.

- While the tea steeps, in a medium bowl, whisk the flour, baking powder, salt, and cinnamon together to blend. In a large bowl, whisk the eggs, sugar, and vanilla until well blended. Squeeze all excess liquid from the tea bags into the milk, discard the bags, then add the milk to the egg mixture in a slow, steady stream, whisking until combined. Using a rubber spatula, fold the flour mixture into the egg mixture, stirring until just incorporated. Add the melted butter, and mix until just blended. (It's OK if a few streaks of butter remain.)

- Pour the batter into the prepared pan and bake for 25 to 35 minutes, or until the cake is puffed and golden and just beginning to brown at the edges. Cool in the pan for 5 to 10 minutes.

- While the cake cools, make the glaze: Combine all the ingredients in a small saucepan and bring to a simmer, stirring until the sugar dissolves, 2 to 3 minutes. Simmer for another 2 minutes, then remove and discard the tea bag. Run a small knife around the edge of the cake, invert it onto a cooling rack, then invert it again onto a platter. Brush half the glaze over the hot cake. Let it sit for a few minutes to soak in the glaze, then brush the remaining glaze over the cake.

- Serve the cake warm or at room temperature, or wrap the cooled cake in plastic wrap and store at room temperature for up to 2 days before serving.

FRAN'S GOLD BAR BROWNIES

recipe by **Fran Bigelow, of Fran's Chocolates**

Across Union Street, just south of the Pike Place Market, Fran's Chocolates is world renowned for its decadent truffles and caramels. Its Gold Bars–gooey caramel and almonds, all wrapped in dark chocolate–set the standard for an adult candy bar. These brownies capitalize on the flavor combination, but they're made with store-bought caramel sauce, so when you wake up at 3 a.m. craving them, you can hit the local twenty-four-hour grocery and get baking instead of waiting for Fran's to open.

A similar version of this recipe was published in *Pure Chocolate,* Fran's Chocolates' definitive guide to baking with chocolate.

active time **40 minutes** | *makes* **24 brownies**

Butter or baking spray for greasing the pan
½ pound (about 3 cups) whole almonds
1 pound semisweet chocolate
1½ ounces unsweetened chocolate, finely chopped
¾ cup (1½ sticks) unsalted butter, at room temperature
¾ cup plus 2 tablespoons (packed) light brown sugar
⅔ cup sugar
1½ teaspoons vanilla extract
3 large eggs
1¾ cups cake flour, sifted before measuring
1 cup caramel sauce, such as Fran's Classic Caramel

- Position a rack in the center of the oven, then preheat the oven to 325°F. Lightly butter a 9-by-13-inch baking pan or similar high-edged sheet pan, and set aside.

- Place the almonds on another baking sheet and toast in the oven for 15 to 20 minutes, or until fragrant and lightly browned. Cool, then roughly chop into ¼-inch pieces. Set aside.

- Finely chop three-quarters of the semisweet chocolate and set it aside for melting. Chop the remaining quarter into ¼-inch chunks and set aside. (These will get stirred directly into the finished batter.)

- Place the finely chopped semisweet chocolate and unsweetened chocolate into a double boiler (or a large metal bowl set over a saucepan of barely simmering water) and cook over low heat, stirring constantly. When the chocolate has nearly melted, remove from the heat and stir until smooth.

- In the work bowl of a stand mixer fitted with the paddle attachment (or using a hand mixer), cream the butter, brown sugar, and sugar on medium speed for 3 to 4 minutes, until light and very fluffy. Stir in the vanilla.

- Add the eggs, one at a time, beating well between additions and scraping the bowl as needed. With the machine on low speed, pour in the reserved melted chocolate, then increase speed to medium and beat for about 15 seconds.

- Remove the bowl from the mixer and fold in the sifted flour by hand until no traces of it remain. (The batter will be quite thick.) Fold in the reserved toasted almonds and chocolate chunks, then spread the batter into the buttered pan in an even layer.

- Spoon the caramel sauce over the top in tablespoon-size dollops. Draw a table knife back and forth through the batter and the caramel, swirling the caramel into the batter a bit. Bake for 45 minutes, or until a toothpick inserted into the brownie section comes out with moist crumbs attached.

- Let the brownies cool in the pan for 1 hour. (Really, try to wait. They're fragile when they're hot.) Cut them into 24 squares and remove the squares with a spatula. Store the brownies in a sealed plastic container for up to 1 week, or cool completely, wrap well, and freeze for up to 2 months.

LAVENDER SHORTBREAD

At Le Panier, the French bakery at the heart of the Pike Place Market, you may be tempted to walk straight to the display case, where *pain au chocolat*, plain and almond *croissants*, and other *viennoiseries* of all shapes and sizes beckon even the weakest sweet tooth. Go, but on the way reach your right hand out to the side and catch a bag of Panier's tender *sablés*, or French shortbread cookies, to take home. This version, made with the lavender that blankets parts of northwestern Washington each summer, is similar.

Look for culinary-grade lavender and resist the temptation to add more—a little goes a long way.

active time **25 minutes** | *makes* **about 3 dozen cookies**

1 cup (2 sticks) unsalted butter, at
    room temperature
¼ cup sugar
¼ cup confectioners' sugar
½ teaspoon vanilla extract
¼ teaspoon kosher salt
1 teaspoon dried lavender, finely
    chopped
2 cups all-purpose flour

- In the work bowl of a stand mixer fitted with the paddle attachment (or using a hand mixer), cream the butter, sugar, and confectioners' sugar on medium speed until light and fluffy, 3 to 4 minutes. Add the vanilla, salt, and lavender, and mix again.

- Add the flour one cup at a time, mixing on low speed between additions until just combined, and scraping the sides of the mixing bowl when necessary. When all the flour has been added, use a plastic spatula to scrape the sides and bottom of the bowl again, and mix briefly.

- Transfer the dough to a board or a clean countertop dusted with flour. Gently knead the dough 5 or 6 times, until it comes together (it should feel sticky). Shape the dough into a long log about 1½ inches in diameter (a square log will work fine too). Wrap the log in plastic wrap and refrigerate until very firm, about 3 hours or overnight. (The dough can also be well wrapped and frozen for up to 1 month.)

- Preheat the oven to 300°F. Line 2 large baking sheets with parchment paper. Slice the dough log into ¼-inch-thick pieces and place the cookies about ¾ inch apart on the baking sheets. Bake for 20 minutes, rotating the sheets from top to bottom and end to end halfway through baking, until the cookies are firm and just barely beginning to brown at the edges.

- Let the cookies cool for 5 minutes on the baking sheets, then transfer them carefully to racks to cool completely. Store the shortbread in airtight containers for up to 1 week.

BUTTERNUT SQUASH BREAD PUDDING

recipe by **Chester "Chet" Gerl, of Matt's in the Market**

When you grab a seat at the bar at Matt's in the Market, known for its sandwiches at lunch, look for the specials board. Filled with dishes inspired by the Market, like this unctuous fall dessert, it usually holds my favorites. Top the pudding with ice cream (Matt's often uses a homemade pecan-mace variety) and caramel sauce, and you've got a recipe for a happy crowd.

Mace is a spice made from grinding the outside covering of a nutmeg seed; it has a similar–but not identical–flavor. Substitute nutmeg in a pinch. Also, if you can't find brioche, challah will work, but because of its light, airy texture, brioche is really the best choice for this recipe.

active time **20 minutes** | *makes* **12 servings**

1 pound ½-inch cubes butternut squash (from a roughly 2-pound squash)
1½ cups heavy cream, divided
¾ cup sugar
2 tablespoons unsalted butter, cut into small cubes, plus more for buttering the dish
¾ teaspoon ground mace
6 large eggs
1 (24-ounce) loaf brioche, cut into ¾-inch cubes

- Preheat the oven to 350°F.

- Arrange the squash on a parchment-lined baking sheet and bake on the middle oven rack for 30 minutes. The squash will be softer but not completely cooked through. Transfer the squash to a small bowl and set aside. Turn the oven off (the bread will need to sit to absorb all the liquid).

- While the squash bakes, in a small saucepan, heat 1 cup of the cream and the sugar over medium heat, stirring frequently, until you see tiny bubbles around the edges of the cream, 2 to 3 minutes. Remove the pan from the heat; stir in the remaining ½ cup cream, 2 tablespoons butter, and mace; set aside.

- In medium bowl, whisk the eggs to blend. Add the reserved cream mixture to the eggs in a slow, steady stream, whisking continuously until all the cream has been added. Place the bread cubes in a large mixing bowl, pour the batter over them, and very gently turn the cubes once or twice to distribute the liquid evenly. Let the bread sit for at least 1 hour (or overnight).

- Preheat the oven to 350°F again. Butter a 9-by-13-inch baking dish (or similar), and transfer half the bread mixture to the dish. Scatter half the squash over the bread, then add the remaining bread, then add the remaining squash. Cover tightly with buttered aluminum foil and bake for 30 minutes. Remove the foil and bake about 10 minutes more, or until the bread is lightly browned and puffed in the center. Let the pudding cool for 10 minutes before serving.

NECTARINE, BLUEBERRY,
and CANDIED HAZELNUT CRISP

If you call something a crisp, there's a high chance people will think it should be eaten for dessert. Do me a favor: don't be afraid to eat it for breakfast, because it's really best first thing in the morning, with a big scoop of Greek yogurt and a strong cup of coffee. The topping on this version (and there's plenty of it) is made with candied Washington hazelnuts—I use the sweet, cinnamon-strong variety from Pike Place Nuts (mostly because it gives me an excuse to buy a whole bag each time I'm blanketed with the aroma from its roasting ovens), but any candied nut will work. The nuts' tough candy shell can make them tricky to chop—smash them with the side of a large knife, like you would for garlic, if you're having trouble.

If you use frozen blueberries, add an extra tablespoon of flour to the fruit mixture.

active time **25 minutes** | *makes* **8 servings**

for the **fruit**

Vegetable oil spray or butter, for the pan
¼ cup all-purpose flour
⅓ cup sugar
½ teaspoon ground cinnamon
1½ pounds juicy, ripe nectarines, pitted and cut into 1-inch chunks
1 pint fresh blueberries (or 2 cups frozen)

for the **topping**

¾ cup all-purpose flour
¾ cup old-fashioned oats
¾ cup (packed) light brown sugar
1 cup candied hazelnuts or other candied nuts, chopped
¾ teaspoon ground cinnamon
6 tablespoons (¾ stick) unsalted butter, melted

- Preheat the oven to 375°F.

- Spray an 8-by-8-inch baking dish lightly with vegetable oil spray and set aside.

- First, make the fruit: Stir the flour, sugar, and cinnamon together in a large mixing bowl. Add the nectarines and blueberries, and gently stir until the fruit is well coated with the flour. Transfer the fruit to the prepared dish, place the dish on a baking sheet to catch any stray drips, and bake on the oven's middle rack for 15 minutes.

- While the fruit bakes, make the crisp topping (you can use the same big bowl): Mix the flour, oats, brown sugar, nuts, and cinnamon together in the bowl, using your hands to break up any clumps of brown sugar, if needed. Pour the melted butter over the dry ingredients and mix until all the dry ingredients are moistened.

- Scatter the topping in an even layer over the fruit, and bake the crisp for an additional 30 minutes, or until the top is nicely browned and the filling is bubbling. Cool the crisp for at least 10 minutes before serving.

WHAT HAPPENS AT LE PANIER *Before You Wake Up*

It's a given: if you walk past the corner of Pike Place and Stewart Street, where Le Panier, which bills itself as a "very French bakery," has been enveloping people with the smell of hot croissants since 1983, you will get hungry. Inside, racks of freshly baked baguettes and specialty breads line the walls. The pastry cases are filled with tarts, *macarons*, éclairs, meringues, filled croissants, palmiers (also known as elephant ears), and simple Parisian-style sandwiches. A stop at Le Panier is a great way to start a morning at Pike Place Market—but for its bakers, the day starts hours before.

Le Panier's goal is simple: It wants to bake as many breads and pastries as possible as close as possible to the time they're consumed. Since its best-selling baguettes and croissants depend on an early-morning dance between seven or eight bakers, four giant ovens, and two convection ovens, timing is tight—and French baker Christian Verbrugghe, a ten-year Le Panier veteran, is their conductor.

Around 4:30 each morning, Le Panier's bakers turn up the heat and immediately start baking the dozens and dozens of croissants that have been rising slowly overnight. The pastries are headed for the rack oven, in which a large man could spin around with his arms outstretched. By 5 a.m. on a slow weekday, 160 butter croissants and 120 *pains au chocolat* cool on giant racks, and almost 300 baguettes move from the bakery's three closet-size proofing boxes, which

proof the breads automatically overnight, to the rack ovens.

Meanwhile, starting around 5:30 a.m., the deck ovens—three flat ovens that peek out from behind Le Panier's pastry case—are hard at work baking fresh rosemary bread, whole grain boules, and various *pains de campagne*, big country-style whole wheat loaves, to a crisp golden brown. Next, the tarts get a turn, and the scent of toasting apples and berries wafts toward the door. Finally, around 7 a.m., the deck ovens are turned over to the pastry bakers, who start rotating batch after batch of éclairs and Le Panier's signature *macarons* through the oven as the store's doors open for business. As people start trickling in, the pastries get ferried down to Le Panier's downstairs pastry production area, where they'll be filled and decorated while the ovens move on to more baguettes and croissants.

As soon as the first baguettes are cool, they get made into Le Panier's French-style sandwiches— the favorites, like ham-and-butter or pâté sandwiches, are refreshingly simple. Usually a line forms quickly, and the aroma of freshly made espresso drinks challenges the baked goods for real estate in your nose. As breakfast goods start flying off the shelves, Christian and the other bakers pour their energy into pastries, filling *macarons* with buttercream and baking the chocolate *sablé* cookies, always temptingly perched in adorable packages for travelers to take home.

And then your alarm goes off. (Don't those croissants taste even better now?)

10 **WAYS** ► *with Bread*

SIMPLE BREAKFAST STRATA
In a large bowl, whisk together 4 large eggs, 1 cup whole milk, ¾ cup half-and-half, salt and pepper to taste, and a handful of chopped fresh herbs. Fill a baking dish with about 4 cups chopped leftover (1-inch) bread cubes. Scatter cooked bacon or sausage, chopped leftover vegetables, and a generous cupful of grated cheese over the top. Pour egg mixture over, soak overnight, and bake for about 45 minutes at 350°F.

BREAKFAST BREAD FRENCH TOAST
Soak sliced banana, zucchini, or lemon poppy seed bread (or Chocolate Chunk Banana Coffee Cake with Pike Place Roast Streusel on page 84) in a mixture of 2 large eggs, 1 cup milk or cream, and ground cinnamon or ginger, then cook on a buttered griddle over medium heat.

MAPLE-CINNAMON TOAST
A new take on the classic: drizzle generously buttered hot toast with maple syrup, then sprinkle with ground cinnamon.

SPICY BUCATINI *with* KALE, SUN-DRIED TOMATOES, *and* BREAD CRUMBS
Sauté 1 packed cup finely chopped kale in 1 tablespoon olive oil with a pinch of crushed red pepper flakes. Add a dime-size bundle of bucatini or spaghetti that's been cooked al dente, 2 tablespoons chopped (oil-packed) sun-dried tomatoes, and 1 tablespoon toasted bread crumbs, and serve with Parmesan cheese. This makes an excellent lunch for one.

OPEN-FACED TUNA SANDWICHES
Mix a can of oil-packed tuna with olive oil, lemon juice, salt and pepper to taste, parsley, and chopped juicy tomatoes. Pile the mixture onto slices of toasted thick-cut bread and serve with a green salad for lunch.

HOMEMADE CROUTONS

Cut half a day-old baguette into ¾-inch pieces (about 6 cups total), then toss with ⅓ cup olive oil and salt and pepper to taste until evenly moist. Bake at 400°F for 10 minutes, or until crisp and brown. (You can also add chopped garlic or herbs to the mixture.)

HOLIDAY STUFFING *for a* SMALLER CROWD

Chop 2 small leeks (white and green parts), 2 ribs celery, and 2 cloves garlic, and sauté them over medium heat in 2 tablespoons butter, until soft. Season to taste with salt and pepper, and 1 tablespoon chopped sage or rosemary. Add ½ cup white wine and simmer, then toss with Homemade Croutons (above), ¾ cup chicken broth, and ½ stick melted butter. Bake at 375°F for 20 minutes, covered, then 15 minutes uncovered.

SPANISH TOASTS *with* GOAT CHEESE, TOMATOES, *and* PAPRIKA OIL

Heat ½ cup olive oil over low heat with ½ teaspoon *pimentón de la Vera* (smoked Spanish paprika; see page 75 for where to purchase). Brush thick-sliced bread with the olive oil and toast at 400°F for 5 minutes, until browned on one side. Flip, spread each toast with goat cheese, sprinkle with chopped tomatoes, and bake a few more minutes, until the cheese melts. Season to taste with salt and pepper and serve.

GRILLED CORNBREAD "SHORTCAKE"

Brush sliced cornbread on both sides with melted butter. Grill over medium heat until toasted, then serve with sliced strawberries and whipped cream.

CHOCOLATE-CARAMEL-BANANA SANDWICH

Slather one piece of bread with store-bought caramel (or even better, salted caramel). Scatter chocolate chips and banana slices over the caramel, and top with another slice of bread. Butter the outside of the bread and toast the sandwich in a panini press or small skillet until the chocolate melts.

FROM *the* CELLAR

RECIPE LIST

GRIST FOR THE MILL:
Beer from Start to Finish, at The Pike Brewing Company

If you're walking down the hallway that leads south from the old Economy Market Building toward Union Street, and you notice a man in rubber boots banging on a giant red silo with a big wooden oar, get closer and start sniffing: you've arrived at The Pike Brewing Company when the brewers are working. The Pike, which was one of the country's smallest breweries when it opened in 1989, still makes all its beer on-site. But this isn't your typical brewing warehouse. Take a seat at one of the high tables overlooking the brewing kettle, which steams away right in the center of The Pike Pub, the brewery's restaurant, and you'll have a good view up a diamond-plated spiral staircase to the grist case—the red silo that holds milled grain—where the banging is coming from. If brewing were a spectator sport, The Pike would be its Wrigley Field.

Tours of the brewery aren't scheduled regularly, but ask in the pub, and they'll find someone to show you around. When I arrive, assistant head brewer Dean Mochizuki takes me down to the basement, where grain is milled and beers are fermented and bottled. The brewery door opens, and I'm greeted with a flood of sweet, malty air. We wind our way up the staircase, right through the center of the pub, to meet Adam Palmer, a mop-headed brewer whose thick-framed glasses look awfully conservative for a beer expert, until you notice they have flames on the temples. Adam is the booted guy with the oar, and like all the brewers, he's on a schedule, performing each detail of the brewing process with an engineer's precision. Today, he's in the middle of brewing Pike Dry Wit, a seasonal white ale that the Pike releases each May. He's just started the mash-in process, where 1,200 pounds of milled grain and 50 pounds of rolled oats are added to a 930-gallon tank called a mash tun, along with 161-degree (not 162-degree) water. Over the course of about twenty minutes, he adds the grain more or less quickly, depending on how the mixture in the tank looks, carefully watching the scale that measures how much grain is left. It's ironic that making something so intrinsically linked with losing track of time requires such accurate timing.

It's also ironic that the nature of our drinking laws means that small boys don't grow up wanting to be beer brewers, because Adam's job is a twelve-year-old's dream. In the mash tun's control tower alone—looking down, you can see through the floor to the pub, and certain people might be tempted to spit—there's what looks like a steering wheel (which controls how much grain spills out into the mash tun), that oar (for knocking stubborn grain into the funnel-shaped bottom of the grist case), and roughly ten million buttons and gauges. When the grain has all been added, and Adam has somehow manipulated all the different control gadgets, he takes me on a tour.

We start back downstairs at the mill, where fresh malted barley drops through a giant hopper and onto a small and very squeaky conveyer belt, which takes it to the gristmill. There, the grains' hulls are cracked open, revealing the starch that will be converted into sugar and then alcohol. The milled grain then takes a trip on a bucket elevator—imagine a small, metal Ferris wheel that only goes up—to the grist case, where we started. After the grain is mashed in, it percolates in the brewing kettle (the tank right in the pub) for about 75 minutes, where it becomes wort. At this point, Adam will add hops—nugget and Cascade hops, in this case. From there, the 200-degree wort heads back down to the basement of the brewery.

The fermentation room is a labyrinth of tanks and hoses. There are so many valves and knobs from floor to ceiling that I'm momentarily convinced the brewery was used as a set for *The Hunt for Red October*, until Adam explains that most of them enable the brewery to wash and sanitize each tank without carting around pressurized hoses—he says sanitization is about 75 percent of his job. While his thirty-barrel batch of Wit boils away one floor up in the brewing kettle, Adam shows me why he's wearing boots—and why you should, too, if you plan to ask for a tour.

After the boiled wort gets recirculated in a tank they call the whirlpool, allowing the brewing kettle to be refilled with another batch of beer-to-be, it gets cooled in a heat exchanger to about 70 degrees, aerated with medical-grade oxygen, and pumped into a fermentation tank, along with live yeast. And every time the beer moves from one apparatus to another, said apparatus gets a full scrub-down. Adam takes time away from cleaning his fermentation tank to spray a new trainee with a high-pressure hose—these folks are detail-oriented, but I wouldn't call them high-strung. After about a week of fermentation (depending on the brew), the Wit will be filtered, chilled to about 33 degrees, carbonated, and then bottled at a mind-blowing rate of forty-eight bottles each minute.

Walking back up to the pub, I'm a little overwhelmed. I've never prided myself on my knack for molecular biology, but Adam explained the brewing process in terms basic enough for a nonbrewer to understand yet detailed enough for me to, well, drink in about as much knowledge as I could take.

Better wash it down with a pint.

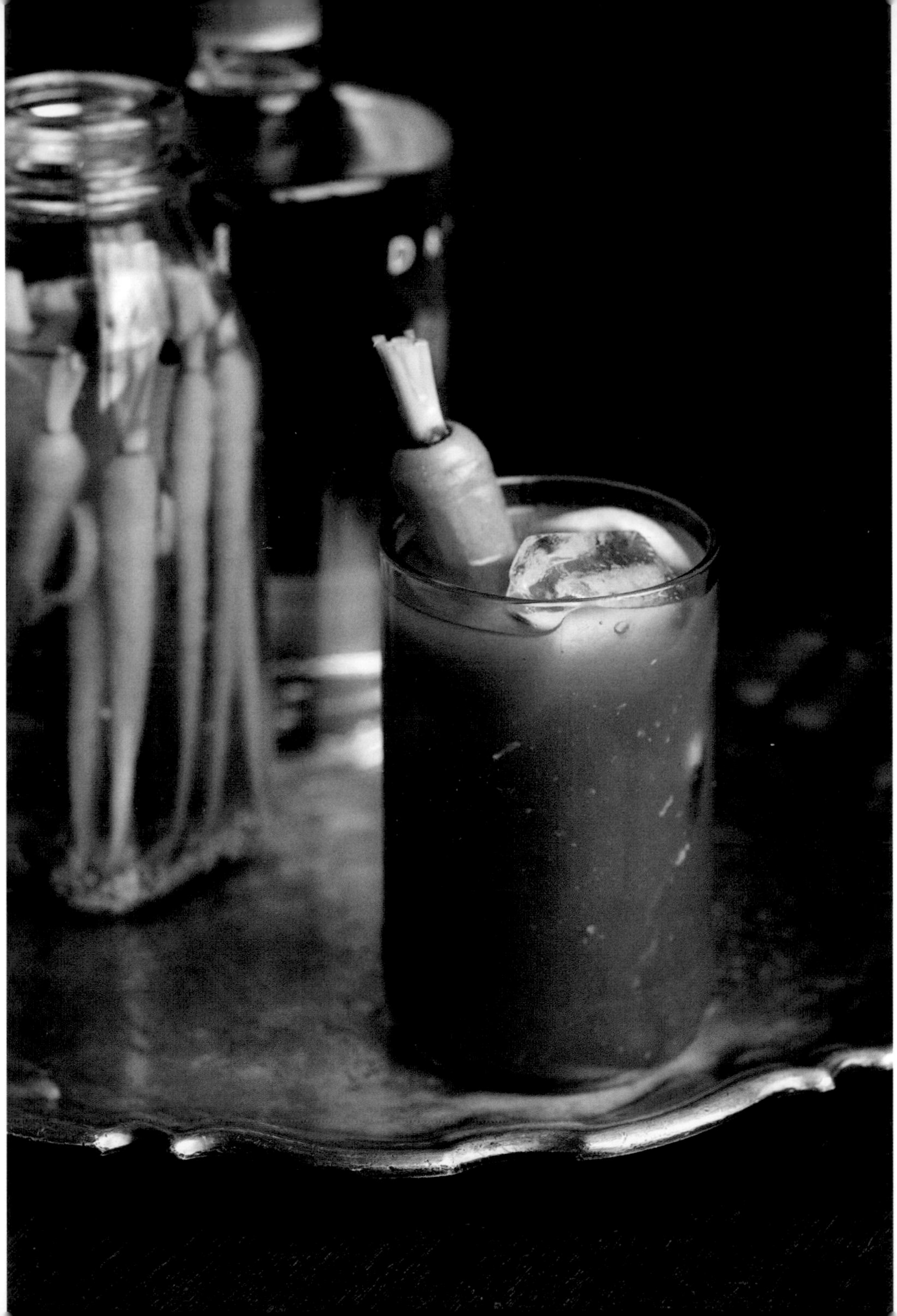

ETTA'S SCRATCH BLOODY MARY
with PICKLED CARROTS

recipe by **Tom Douglas, of Etta's**

Made with pepper-infused vodka and freshly grated horseradish, a stellar Bloody Mary tops off the Market-inspired brunch at Etta's. There, they serve them with a spear of pickled asparagus, but a carrot is a great change of pace. Look for multicolored heirloom carrots–the kind that come with the greens on–for a great presentation.

active time **30 minutes for pickling, plus 5 minutes per drink** | *makes* **6 drinks**

6 cups tomato juice
7½ ounces (about 1 cup) pepper-
   infused vodka
1½ teaspoons freshly grated
   horseradish
1½ teaspoons Worcestershire sauce
Tabasco sauce
Celery salt
Freshly ground black pepper
1 lemon, cut into wedges
6 Pickled Carrots (recipe follows)

■ For each drink, fill a cocktail shaker halfway with small ice cubes. Add 1 cup of the tomato juice, 1¼ ounces vodka, ¼ teaspoon each of grated horseradish and Worcestershire sauce, plus a dash of Tabasco and pinch of celery salt to taste, and a grinding of pepper. Put the top on and shake. Pour into a large ice-filled glass. Squeeze in and add the lemon wedge, garnish with a pickled carrot, and serve immediately.

PICKLED CARROTS

makes **2 pounds pickled carrots**

2 cups apple cider vinegar
2 cups water
2 tablespoons mustard seeds
1 tablespoon plus 1 teaspoon whole
  coriander seeds
1 tablespoon plus 1 teaspoon black
  peppercorns
¼ cup kosher salt
¼ cup plus 2 tablespoons sugar
1 shallot, thinly sliced
2 pounds carrots

- Combine the vinegar, water, mustard seeds, coriander seeds, peppercorns, salt, sugar, and shallot in a large, nonreactive saucepan. Bring to a simmer, reduce heat to low, and simmer for 20 minutes, stirring occasionally. Set the pickling liquid aside and let cool to room temperature.

- While the liquid cools, cut the greens from the carrot tops, leaving about ½ inch of stem, then peel the carrots.

- Fill a large, wide saucepan with about 1 inch of water and bring to a simmer. Cook the carrots for 3 to 4 minutes, leaving them slightly crunchy. While the carrots cook, fill a large bowl with ice water. Drain the carrots, then shock them in the ice water. Drain again.

- Combine the blanched carrots and pickling liquid in a sealable container, so that the vegetables are fully submerged. (A large zip-top bag works well.) Let sit, refrigerated, for at least 2 days, or up to 2 weeks, before serving.

IL BISTRO'S GUIDO CONTINI

recipe by **David Nelson, of Il Bistro**

At the bottom of the cobbled drive that wanders under the Pike Place Market sign, near the Market Theater, Il Bistro serves classic Italian fare in a cozy setting—think rich red tones, dark wood, arched doorways, and a bar lined with unique scotches, cognacs, and grappas. The food's great, but you'll come back first for a perfectly crafted cocktail, as people have been doing since 1975. David Nelson, the bar manager, named this cocktail in homage to the lead character in the Fellini movie *8½:* a film director addicted to gin, obsessed with women (represented by chocolate and cherries), and constantly smoking (hence the scotch).

There's only enough scotch to give it a whiff of smoke, but it makes the drink—so use the good stuff. At Il Bistro, the drink is garnished with brandied cherries.

active time **5 minutes** | *makes* **1 drink**

1½ ounces London dry gin
1 ounce Carpano Antica Formula vermouth
½ ounce dark crème de cacao
2 dashes angostura bitters
1 dash Laphroaig 10-year-old scotch or other good-quality smoky scotch
2 brandied cherries

- Fill a cocktail shaker half full with ice. Add the gin, vermouth, crème de cacao, bitters, and scotch, and shake well. Strain the liquid into a cold glass and serve immediately, garnished with brandied cherries.

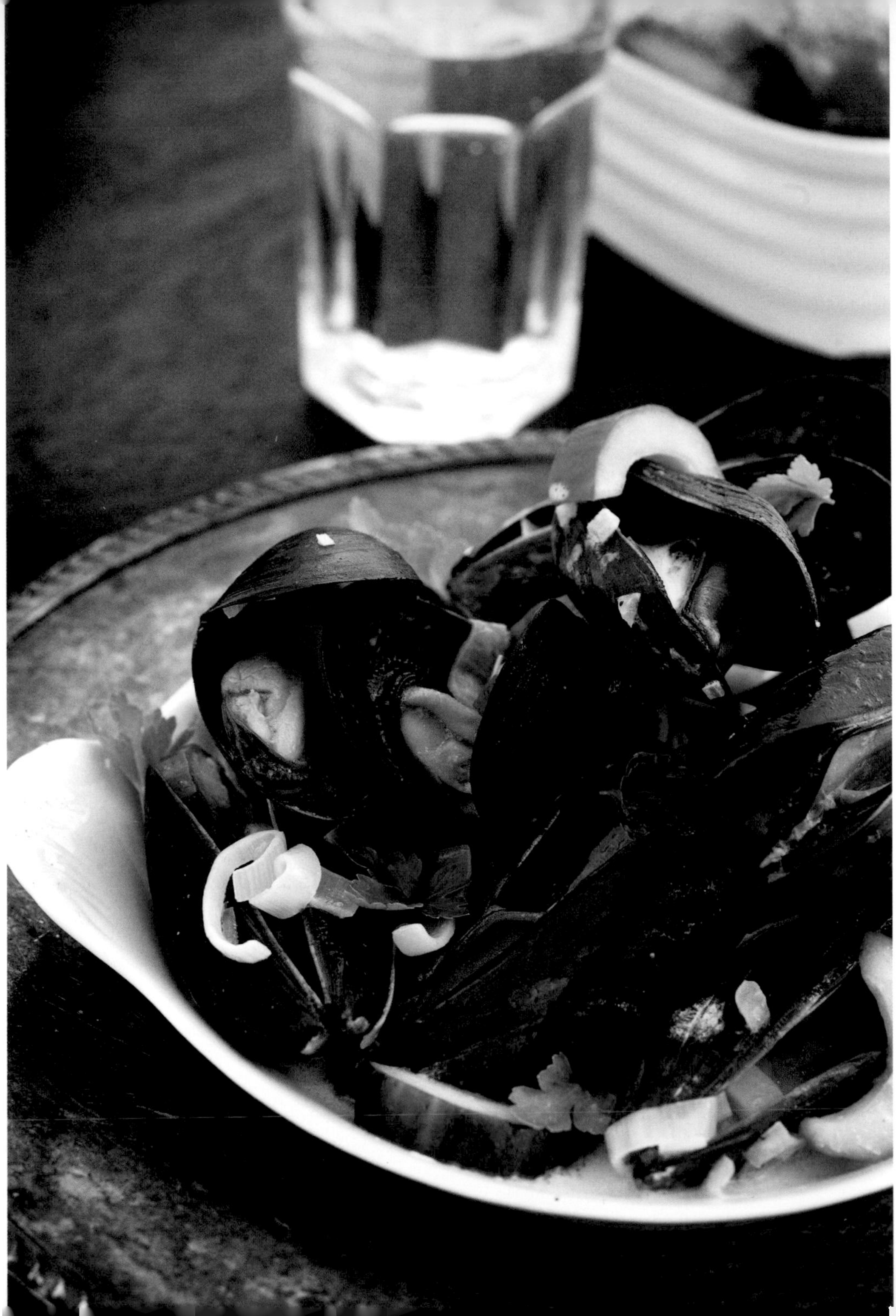

MARCHÉ'S MUSSELS *with* PERNOD CREAM

recipe by **Randy Whiteford, of Marché**

Marché (formerly Campagne)—the French restaurant on Pine Street at the Inn at the Market, the Pike Place Market's only hotel—is known for timeless dishes, executed perfectly, often with a twist. However, chef Daisley Gordon's team is constantly revamping the menu, providing diners with French classics that stray just a bit from the cuisine, like this mussel dish, made with cucumbers and a Pernod-spiked cream sauce. It only has a hint of anise, but the effect is sublime.

active time **25 minutes** | *makes* **4 servings**

¾ large English cucumber
¼ cup extra-virgin olive oil
1 small shallot, finely chopped
1 heaping tablespoon finely chopped
 onion
1 medium leek, halved lengthwise,
 washed, and cut into ¼-inch half
 moons
2 pounds mussels, cleaned
Kosher salt and freshly ground black
 pepper
¼ cup Pernod
½ cup dry white wine
1 cup heavy cream
¼ cup (½ stick) unsalted butter,
 cut into tablespoons, at room
 temperature
Juice of ½ medium lemon (about 1½
 tablespoons)
¼ cup chopped Italian parsley
1 baguette, sliced and toasted

- Peel the cucumber, then cut it in half lengthwise. Scoop the seeds out with a small spoon or a melon baller, and cut the cucumber into ¼-inch-thick half moons. Set aside.

- Heat a large, wide soup pot or Dutch oven with a tight-fitting lid over medium heat. When hot, add the olive oil, then the shallot, onion, and leek, and sauté until they just begin to soften, about 3 to 4 minutes. Add the mussels and stir to coat evenly with the oil. Season to taste with salt and pepper, then add the Pernod and white wine and simmer for 1 minute. Add the cream, cover the pot, and let the mussels cook for 5 to 10 minutes, until all the mussels have opened (discard any that don't).

- Once all the mussels have opened, add the reserved cucumber and the butter, and stir the mixture until the butter has melted. Add the lemon juice, then taste the sauce and season, if necessary, with additional salt and pepper. Transfer the finished mussels to a serving bowl, sprinkle with the chopped parsley, and serve hot, with the baguette slices.

SCOTCH-SPIKED CHICKEN LIVER PÂTÉ

At Le Pichet, the classic French bistro near the corner of First and Virginia, the perfect lunch starts with a charcuterie plate. To order, glance up at the chalkboard—there is invariably a great European cured meat selection, along with such house-made specialties as pork rillettes and clove-spiked *pâté de campagne*. My favorite is Le Pichet's *gâteau aux foie de volailles*, a smooth chicken liver terrine. Served in a slab sprinkled with *fleur de sel*, it's almost unreasonably creamy—perfect pressed into a baguette hunk slathered with mustard, topped simply with a slice of cornichon.

In this simpler version, chicken livers are simmered in a mixture of chardonnay and scotch with white peppercorns and cloves, then whipped into a soft pâté perfect for spreading on crackers or baguette slices. Serve with cornichons and French mustard, and perhaps a glass of pinot noir.

active time **30 minutes** | *makes* **two 2-cup portions, or appetizers for a crowd**

1 large shallot, thinly sliced
1 large clove garlic, smashed
1 cup dry chardonnay
⅔ cup plus 2 tablespoons good-quality smoky scotch
3 whole cloves
3 whole white peppercorns
1 pound chicken livers, fat and veins trimmed away
2 sticks unsalted butter, cut into tablespoons, at room temperature
Sea salt
Ground white pepper

- Combine the shallot, garlic, chardonnay, ⅔ cup scotch, cloves, and peppercorns in a large, wide saucepan and bring to a simmer. Cook for 5 to 10 minutes, until the garlic is soft. Add the chicken livers, bring back to a bare simmer, and cook, turning the livers once or twice, for about 5 minutes more, or until they're barely pink in the center. Remove the pan from the heat and let it sit, covered, for 15 minutes.

- Using a slotted spoon, carefully transfer the livers, shallot, and garlic to a food processor, picking out any spices as you see them. Discard the liquid. Add the remaining 2 tablespoons scotch to the livers, then puree the liver mixture until smooth.

- With the machine on, add the butter one chunk at a time and puree until smooth, scraping the sides of the work bowl as necessary. Season to taste with sea salt and white pepper. Pass the pâté through a fine-mesh strainer into a bowl, then transfer to a large, shallow serving dish or two small bowls. Let the pâté cool to room temperature, then refrigerate overnight, with the surface covered *directly* with plastic wrap. Serve chilled.

NOTE: The pâté can be cooled and covered with a thin layer of melted butter, then double-wrapped and frozen for up to 2 weeks before serving. Thaw for 24 to 48 hours in the refrigerator, then serve.

ALE-BRAISED BRATWURST
with **APPLE SAUERKRAUT** *and* **STOUT MUSTARD**

recipe by **Gary Marx, of The Pike Pub**

The Pike Pub is tucked into a basement just south of the Market. It's known for beers like the sensationally dark Extra Stout, a rich stout; the malty, smoky, Scotch-style Kilt Lifter; and the yeasty tripel ale Monk's Uncle. It's also known for its food–the bratwurst can't be missed.

For his brats and sauerkraut, Pike Pub chef Gary Marx starts with wurst from the Market's Uli's Famous Sausage: Uli makes brats with Kilt Lifter just for Gary. Gary then braises them in beer and serves them with an apple-spiked sauerkraut and a whole grain mustard made with stout and the same malt extract often used in beer brewing. If you judge it just right, you can buy a 22-ounce bottle of stout, add some to the mustard, drink a bit, and still have enough left to braise the bratwurst.

Look for malt extract at a brewing supply store. If you can't find it, substitute honey.

active time **40 minutes** | *makes* **8 servings**

8 bratwursts
16 ounces ale, such as Pike Brewing
   Company's Pike Pale
Apple Sauerkraut (recipe follows)
Stout Mustard (recipe follows)

- Place the bratwursts in a wide pot or deep skillet. Add the beer (it should almost cover the brats) and cook at a bare simmer over medium heat for about 30 minutes, turning occasionally, until the brats are glazed with beer and most of the liquid has evaporated.

- Serve the brats hot on a bed of hot Apple Sauerkraut, with Stout Mustard alongside for dipping.

APPLE SAUERKRAUT

Sauerkraut is one of life's easiest pleasures, if you don't have to make it yourself from scratch. Here, Gary Marx blends it with the traditional caraway and spikes it with apples, for a decidedly Washingtonian twist.

makes **8 servings**

¼ cup (½ stick) unsalted butter
1 medium brown onion, diced
1 small tart apple, peeled, cored, and chopped
1½ teaspoons whole caraway seeds
2 tablespoons (packed) light brown sugar
2 pounds refrigerated, prepared sauerkraut (one 32-ounce bag), drained
Kosher salt and freshly ground black pepper

- Melt the butter in a large skillet over medium heat. When melted, add the onion and sauté until soft, about 5 minutes. Add the apple and caraway seeds, and cook for another 5 minutes, stirring occasionally. Add the brown sugar and sauerkraut, season to taste with salt and pepper, and simmer over low heat, stirring occasionally, for 10 to 15 minutes, or until the apples begin to disintegrate.

STOUT MUSTARD

Since you'll have extra mustard leftover, plan to serve some alongside Rosemary-Crusted Pork Loin with Balsamic Red Plum Sauce (page 43), Herb-Roasted Red Potatoes (page 187), or atop simply grilled salmon or chicken. This mustard is also yummy on baked potatoes or tossed with steamed green beans.

makes **1½ cups mustard**

¾ cup whole grain mustard
½ cup dark stout, such as Pike Brewing Company's Extra Stout
3 tablespoons (packed) light brown sugar
2 teaspoons apple cider vinegar
1½ tablespoons malt extract

- Combine all the ingredients in a food processor or blender. Pulse to combine, transfer to a small bowl, and refrigerate until ready to serve.

ONE-PAN COQ AU VIN

In its most classic form, coq au vin is a whole chicken, braised in burgundy wine with onions, mushrooms, and bacon. It's heartwarming and stomach satisfying, but between peeling the traditional pearl onions and searing the chicken before braising it, it can take a significant amount of time. This version, made with a syrah from Patterson Cellars, is much simpler. You roast the onions, mushrooms, and bacon in the oven while you prepare the other ingredients, then pop the chicken on top for the remaining baking time–so both the wine lovers and the crispy skin lovers at the table can rejoice. Serve with good crusty bread for mopping up the juices.

Patterson Cellars' tasting room is on the Pike Street Hill Climb, just below the Market on Western Avenue. If you can't stop by for a bottle of its syrah, with its caramel nose and jammy cherry flavors, look for another well-balanced red wine with bold tannins and a relatively heavy mouthfeel.

active time **40 minutes** | *makes* **6 servings**

¼ pound thick-sliced bacon, diced
8 ounces cremini mushrooms, rinsed, trimmed, and halved
1 small onion, halved and thinly sliced
1 tablespoon olive oil
5 large carrots, peeled and chopped into 2-inch pieces
2 large cloves garlic, finely chopped
1 tablespoon plus 2 teaspoons chopped fresh thyme
1 pound golf ball–size red potatoes
Kosher salt and freshly ground black pepper
1½ cups syrah
2 large or 4 small split chicken breasts, bone-in and skin-on (about 2 pounds total), cut in half if large
2 skin-on chicken thighs (about 1 pound)
2 tablespoons chopped fresh parsley
2 tablespoons unsalted butter, cut into 8 pieces

- Preheat the oven to 400°F.

- Scatter the bacon on the bottom of a roasting pan. Add the mushrooms and onion, drizzle with the olive oil, and shake the pan to combine. Roast, stirring halfway through, for 20 minutes, or until the bacon is crisp.

- Add the carrots, garlic, 1 tablespoon of the thyme, and potatoes to the roasting pan, and season to taste with salt and pepper. Stir and roast for another 10 minutes. Increase the oven temperature to 450°F.

- Add the wine to the bottom of the pan, then arrange the chicken pieces on top of everything. Season the chicken to taste with salt and pepper and the remaining 2 teaspoons thyme, then bake for 30 to 40 minutes more, until the skin is crisp and the chicken is cooked through.

- To serve, place a piece of chicken in each of 6 large, shallow bowls. Add the parsley and butter to the pan and stir until the butter melts, then spoon vegetables and sauce into the bowls next to the chicken. Serve immediately.

LINGUINE ALLA VONGOLE

recipe by **Jacqueline Roberts, of The Pink Door**

If you make reservations for dinner at The Pink Door, the unsigned (but aptly named) Italian comfort-food haven off Post Alley that's been serving traditional hearty fare since 1981, you should probably be ready for anything: the food is paired with cabaret entertainment, ranging from saxophone players to burlesque dancers. Jacqueline Roberts, the owner, is sometimes reluctant to give up her old family recipes. It's no wonder, when simple Italian favorites like linguine and clams are served studded with pancetta and laced with white wine, chili, and lemon zest. Although delicious at home, this dish somehow tastes decidedly different in the restaurant. You know the old saying—nothing enhances the dining experience like a trapeze artist overhead.

active time **30 minutes** | *makes* **4 to 6 servings**

1¾ pounds manila clams
½ cup chopped pancetta
1 pound linguine
½ cup extra-virgin olive oil, plus more for drizzling, if desired
2 tablespoons finely chopped fresh oregano
Grated zest of 2 medium lemons (about 2 tablespoons)
¼ to ½ teaspoon crushed red pepper flakes
4 large cloves garlic, finely chopped
1½ cups dry white wine
1½ tablespoons unsalted butter, cut into small pieces
½ cup finely chopped fresh parsley
Kosher salt and freshly ground black pepper

- Place the clams in a bowl. Add cold water to cover and set aside; the clams will siphon out any sand and grit.

- Bring a large pot of salted water to a boil for the pasta.

- Heat a large lidded skillet over medium heat. Add the pancetta and cook, stirring occasionally, for 6 to 8 minutes, or until browned. (If the water hasn't come to a boil at this point, turn the heat under the pan off and let the pancetta sit until the water boils.)

- When the water boils, cook the linguine al dente according to package instructions. Drain and set aside.

- While the pasta cooks, return the skillet to medium heat. Add the olive oil, oregano, lemon zest, red pepper flakes, and garlic, and sauté for about a minute. Add the wine and bring to a simmer. Drain and rinse the clams, and add them to the pan. Cover and let cook for 5 minutes, or until all the clams have opened. Discard any unopened clams, and let the clams simmer on low heat until the pasta is ready.

- When the pasta is done, scatter the butter over the clams, then add the drained pasta, parsley, and salt and pepper to taste. Using tongs, transfer the pasta into 4 to 6 warm bowls, and pour the clams and sauce over the top. Drizzle with additional extra-virgin olive oil (use your best oil here) and serve immediately.

BEER-BRAISED BRISKET
with GLAZED CARROTS *and* PARSNIPS

Pear Delicatessen & Shoppe has a beer selection that smites any beer lover in a glance. Here's a recipe that gives you another excuse to shop there: start with a rich, strong beer (one with a bit of sweetness, like a winter ale or stout), good beef broth, and a well-trimmed brisket, and you'll end up with a wintry meal that warms your body to the core.

To make the brisket a day ahead (which, honestly, makes it taste better), let the beef cool to room temperature in its braising liquid after it comes out of the oven, and refrigerate it overnight. Before serving, skim any fat off the surface of the sauce, then proceed with simmering and cooking the vegetables. Slice the beef cold and reheat it in the finished sauce, then serve it over mashed potatoes, couscous, or polenta—my favorite is a mashed mix of potatoes and sweet potatoes.

NOTE: This recipe can be made with red wine, if you're not a big beer fan (use 1½ cups wine in place of each bottle of beer). In that case, reduce the brown sugar by half to 2 tablespoons.

active time **60 minutes** | *makes* **6 servings**

for the **brisket**

1 (3-pound) beef brisket, trimmed of
    excess fat
Kosher salt and freshly ground black
    pepper
1 tablespoon canola oil
1 small onion, finely chopped
2 cloves garlic, finely chopped
3 whole cloves
1 cinnamon stick
1½ teaspoons dried thyme
2 tablespoons tomato paste
8 ounces cremini mushrooms, rinsed,
    trimmed, and quartered
1 (12-ounce) bottle winter ale or stout
2 cups beef broth
¼ cup (packed) light brown sugar
2 tablespoons chopped fresh parsley

- Preheat the oven to 325°F.

- First, make the brisket: Heat a large, ovenproof heavy-bottomed pot with a tight-fitting lid (such as a Dutch oven) over medium heat. Season the brisket with salt and pepper to taste on both sides. When the pan is hot, add the oil, then sear the brisket for 8 to 10 minutes per side, until very well browned. Transfer the brisket to a plate and set aside. (Depending on the size of your brisket, you may need to cut the meat in half and sear it in two separate batches.)

- Add the onion and sauté for 5 minutes, or until the onion is soft, using a wooden spoon to scrape any brown bits off the bottom of the pan. (You may need to add a tablespoon or two of water if the onion begins to stick to the pan.) Add the garlic, cloves, cinnamon stick, and thyme, season to taste with salt and pepper, and sauté for another minute. Stir in the tomato paste and mushrooms and cook for a few minutes, until the mushrooms begin to lose their water. Add the beer and beef broth and bring to a strong simmer, scraping the pan again to release any good brown bits. As soon as the mixture simmers, slide the beef back in.

for the vegetables

¾ pound (about 5 large) carrots, peeled and chopped into 1-inch pieces

¾ pound (about 3 large) parsnips, peeled and chopped into 1-inch pieces

1½ cups (6 ounces) pearl onions, peeled

1 clove garlic, smashed

3 whole cloves

1 (12-ounce) bottle winter ale or stout

½ cup (packed) light brown sugar

Kosher salt and freshly ground black pepper

- Cover the pot and place it in the oven. Braise the beef for 1 hour, then carefully flip the beef, stir in the brown sugar, and braise for another 1½ to 2 hours, or until a skewer inserted into the center of the beef comes out with absolutely no resistance.

- Transfer the brisket to a large shallow bowl and cover it with aluminum foil. Return the pot to the stove, fish out and discard the cinnamon stick, and cook the sauce at a strong simmer for 10 to 20 minutes, until the liquid has reduced by almost half.

- While the liquid cooks down, make the vegetables: Combine the carrots, parsnips, pearl onions, garlic, cloves, beer, brown sugar, and salt and pepper to taste in a medium saucepan. Bring to a simmer and cook, covered, for 10 minutes. Remove the lid and cook, uncovered, until the beer glazes the vegetables, about 10 minutes more. Remove and discard any cloves you can easily spot, check seasonings, and add additional salt and pepper if needed.

- Slice the beef thinly across the grain and pile onto a bed of mashed potatoes, couscous, or polenta, along with the vegetables and sauce. Top with the parsley and serve immediately.

MARKET TIP: *Peeling Pearl Onions*

To peel pearl onions, first trim the roots and papery tips from the ends. Using a small, sharp knife, make an X in the root end of each onion. Submerge the onions in a small pot of simmering water for 2 minutes, rinse with cool water, then peel. You can also often find prepeeled pearl onions in a grocery store's freezer section. Thaw them before using.

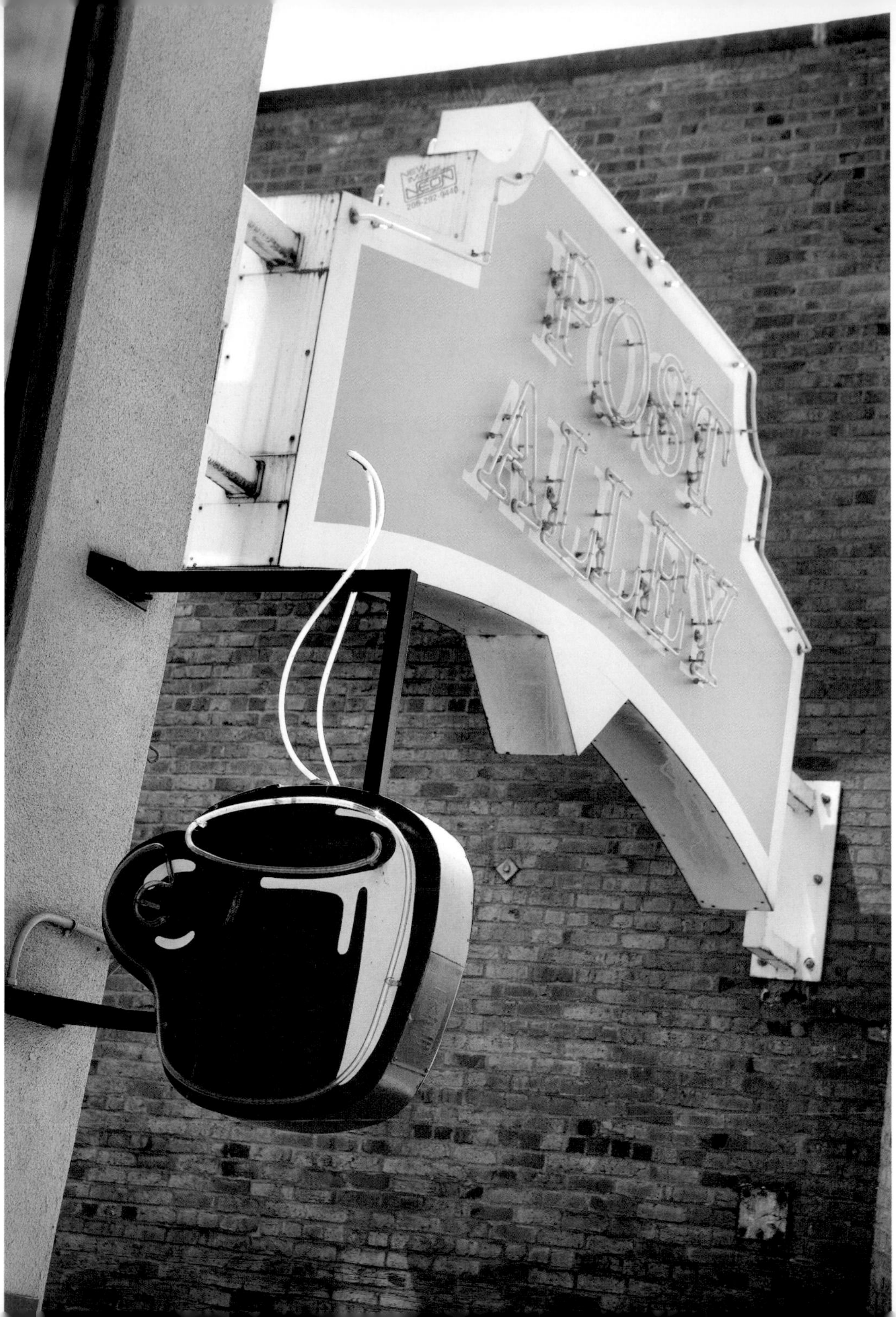
POST
ALLEY

PAN-SEARED ROSEMARY LAMB CHOPS
with DRIED CHERRY WINE SAUCE

based on a recipe by **Brian Klure, of Chukar Cherries**

Chukar Cherries' Dried Totally Tart and Columbia River Tart cherries may be delicious out of hand, but simmered with a few cups of good wine, they make an even better simple pan sauce. If you must use regular dried cherries, omit the sugar.

active time **15 minutes** | *makes* **4 servings**

1 cup dried tart cherries
2½ cups high-quality red wine (syrah, merlot, or pinot noir)
1 tablespoon sugar
8 small lamb chops (each about 1¼ inch thick, 2 generous pounds total), patted dry
1 tablespoon olive oil
2 tablespoons chopped fresh rosemary
Kosher salt and freshly ground black pepper

- Place the cherries and wine in a medium saucepan and bring to a boil over high heat. Reduce the heat to medium and simmer for 20 minutes, or until the liquid is reduced by a bit more than half. Stir in the sugar and set the pan aside; the cherries will plump up more as they sit.

- Heat a large skillet over medium-high heat. Rub the lamb chops on both sides with the olive oil, then season with the rosemary and salt and pepper to taste. Cook for 10 to 12 minutes for medium-rare, turning once, only when the lamb releases easily from the pan. Transfer the seared chops to a serving platter.

- Pour the cherry sauce into the hot pan and simmer for 2 to 3 minutes over high heat, or until the sauce has thickened considerably. Pour the sauce over the hot chops and serve immediately.

ELDERFLOWER CHAMPAGNE COCKTAIL

Because the Pike Place Market is such an amalgam of specialty stores, it's a great place to shop when your list calls for a bunch of things you might not keep on hand–Seattle-made orange bitters, for example (Scrappy's Bitters are available at DeLaurenti), or German elderflower syrup (available at Bavarian Meats). Pike & Western Wine Shop, known for its selection of limited-release Washington wines, always has perfect wine-pairing advice. Pick up a few new pantry essentials, add an extra bottle of bubbly, and start your meal with this simple cocktail.

active time **5 minutes** | *makes* **1 cocktail**

3 to 4 dashes orange bitters (such as
    Scrappy's Bitters)
Scant 1 tablespoon elderflower syrup
½ cup chilled champagne

■ Shake the bitters into the bottom of a champagne glass. Add the elderflower syrup, then the champagne, and serve immediately.

CLASSIC BISCOTTI *with* VIN SANTO

recipe by **Mike Easton, of Il Corvo Pasta**

Here in the United States, biscotti have taken a turn away from Italy, becoming larger, softer, and sweeter than their historic cousins. At Il Corvo, the little pasta joint churning out impeccable house-made pastas in a tiny cafeteria-style space west of the Pike Place Market across Western Avenue, meals sometimes end with firm lemon-scented biscotti and a glass of *vin santo*, a traditional Italian dessert wine that often accompanies true biscotti.

Pike & Western Wine Shop, opened in 1975 by two men who met while campaigning to save the Market from threats to tear it down, has a great selection of sweet Italian wines–try serving these with a traditional *vin santo* from Chianti.

active time **25 minutes** | *makes* **about 3 dozen biscotti**

3½ cups all-purpose flour, plus more
   for forming the biscotti
1 teaspoon baking soda
1 teaspoon baking powder
½ teaspoon kosher salt
Grated zest of 2 medium lemons
   (about 2 tablespoons)
1¼ cups (6 ounces) pine nuts
5 tablespoons unsalted butter, at
   room temperature
1⅔ cups sugar
3 large eggs
1½ teaspoons vanilla extract
Vin santo, for serving

- Preheat the oven to 350°F. Line a baking sheet with parchment paper and set aside.

- In a medium bowl, whisk the flour, baking soda, baking powder, salt, lemon zest, and pine nuts to blend. Set aside.

- In the work bowl of a stand mixer fitted with the paddle attachment (or using a hand mixer), cream the butter and sugar together on low speed for 2 minutes, until the mixture looks like wet sand. Add the eggs, and mix again on medium speed for about a minute. Stir in the vanilla. Add the dry ingredients in three separate additions, mixing on low speed until combined between each addition.

- Transfer the dough to a lightly floured board, kneading it together briefly to incorporate any stray pieces. Divide the dough into two roughly equal sections and form each piece into a flat log about 16 inches long and 2 inches wide, using additional flour, if necessary. Transfer the logs to the prepared baking sheet, leaving at least 3 inches between them, and bake for 20 minutes, or until puffed and golden.

- Remove the biscotti and reduce the oven temperature to 300°F. Let the biscotti cool for 5 to 10 minutes. When they're cool enough to touch comfortably, gently transfer the logs to a cutting board and slice them into ½-inch pieces with a large, serrated knife. (Using a sawing motion prevents the biscotti from tearing as you cut them.) Transfer the biscotti back to the baking sheet, cut sides down, and bake for another 30 minutes, or until firm, turning the biscotti halfway through the second bake. (Depending on how you cut your biscotti, you may need to use an additional parchment-lined baking sheet.)

- Cool biscotti completely before serving with *vin santo* for dipping.

- Cooled biscotti can be stored in a metal tin for up to 2 weeks, or frozen.

PERFECT PAIRINGS

Part wine bar and part wine cave, The Tasting Room sells wines from eight exclusive vintner-owned Washington wineries, none of which produce more than three thousand cases per year. Organized more like a co-op than a retail store, The Tasting Room is legally licensed as a winery—meaning that if you live out of town, they can ship your wine home. Go for a seasonal tasting flight late on Friday afternoon and stay for game night. Or stop in for the wine that pairs perfectly with the recipes below—and know that because they're only sold at the Pike Place Market, most likely none of your guests will show up with the same bottle.

Etta's Mini Dungeness Crab Cakes with Green Cocktail Sauce
Naches Heights Pinot Gris

Grilled Octopus and Chickpea Salad
Mountain Dome Washington State Brut

Braised Baby Back Ribs with Chipotle-Cherry Sauce
Camaraderie Cellars Grace

Pan-Seared Rosemary Lamb Chops with Dried Cherry Wine Sauce
Harlequin Wine Cellars Sundance Vineyard Syrah

Spicy Marinated Feta
Latitude 46 North Dry Gewürztraminer

Orecchiette Pasta with Cauliflower Cream and Shaved Black Truffles
Wilridge Winery Nebbiolo di Klipsun

Beer-Braised Brisket with Glazed Carrots and Parsnips
2007 Wineglass Cellars Cabernet

Rosemary-Crusted Pork Loin with Balsamic Red Plum Sauce
Bunnell Family Cellar Northridge Mourvedre

FROM *the* PANTRY

RECIPE LIST

OUTRAGEOUS GARLIC BREADSTICKS

Swathed in garlic, herbs, Parmesan cheese, butter, and olive oil, these breadsticks are over the top in every way. Eat them like garlic bread right when they come out of the oven, or serve them with soups for dipping and soaking (they are crisp like croutons).

active time **20 minutes** | *makes* **about 10 breadsticks**

1 baguette
½ cup (1 stick) unsalted butter, at room temperature
¼ cup extra-virgin olive oil
1½ tablespoons finely chopped fresh parsley
1 teaspoon finely chopped fresh thyme
2 teaspoons finely chopped fresh rosemary
2 teaspoons finely chopped fresh oregano
2 large cloves garlic, finely chopped
½ teaspoon kosher salt
¼ teaspoon freshly ground black pepper
¼ cup finely grated Parmesan cheese

- Preheat the oven to 400°F. Line a large rimmed baking sheet with aluminum foil and set aside.

- Using a large serrated knife, cut the baguette diagonally (at a roughly 45-degree angle) into ¾-inch-thick slices–you should end up with 9 or 10 (6-inch-long) pieces. Set aside.

- In a small mixing bowl, mash the butter, olive oil, parsley, thyme, rosemary, oregano, garlic, salt, pepper, and Parmesan cheese together until combined. (The butter mixture can be made up to 4 hours ahead, covered, and left at room temperature until ready to use; alternately, you can make it a few days ahead, refrigerate it, and bring it to room temperature before using.)

- Using a small rubber spatula, spread the butter mixture onto both sides of the croutons in a thin, even layer. (You may not quite use all of it.) Place the croutons on the prepared sheet and bake, turning them halfway through, for about 20 minutes, or until they are toasty golden brown on both sides. Drain the croutons briefly on paper towels, then serve warm.

NOTE: Croutons can also be completely assembled, wrapped well in plastic wrap, and frozen for up to 2 weeks. Bake as directed.

HOMEMADE AIOLI

It may sound exotic, but making aioli at home isn't very hard—and (unfortunately for our waistlines, perhaps) it can turn almost anyone into a mayonnaise lover. Use this simple garlicky version as a sandwich slather, or dip roasted potatoes or steamed artichoke leaves in it. For fish recipes, cut the amount of garlic in half and tart the aioli up with 2 tablespoons each finely chopped cornichons, onions, and capers, plus a pinch of cayenne and an extra squeeze of lemon.

Be sure to use eggs from a source you trust; the yolks do not get cooked.

active time **10 minutes (15 minutes if made by hand)** | *makes* **about 1 cup**

4 large egg yolks
2 teaspoons Dijon mustard
½ teaspoon kosher salt
1 teaspoon freshly squeezed lemon
    juice or apple cider vinegar
2 cloves garlic, very finely chopped
1 cup canola oil

- In the work bowl of a stand mixer fitted with the whisk attachment (or in a medium bowl, using a whisk), beat the egg yolks on medium speed until pale in color and very thick, about 3 minutes—when you take the whisk out and allow the yolks to drip off it, the stream should hover on the surface of the yolks for a moment before sinking in. Add the mustard, salt, lemon juice, and garlic, and whisk until well blended. With the machine on medium speed, add the oil one teaspoon at a time until about a third of the oil has been incorporated. Once the aioli starts to look thicker, like a sauce, add the oil in a very slow, steady stream. When all the oil has been incorporated, whisk on medium-high speed until completely emulsified and smooth. Season to taste with additional salt, if necessary, and serve immediately—the aioli does not keep well.

HOMEMADE CHICKEN STOCK

Chicken stock recipes are a dime a dozen, which is a good thing; it's one of the few things I believe everyone should know how to make. Soups and stews made with homemade stock taste better, period. And the tonic smell of stock bubbling away on the stove has curative powers for me.

I make my stock differently every time, depending on what I have in the fridge, but for economic reasons, I tend to use leftover roasted chicken carcasses (as opposed to whole new birds, which some cooks swear by). After roasting a bird, pick away the edible meat (be lazy about the process, so there's still enough meat on the carcass to add flavor to the stock), chop through the spine and each large bone once or twice with a big, heavy knife to expose the bone marrow (which helps give the stock a great mouthfeel), and freeze the chicken in zip-top bags until you're ready to use it.

active time **15 minutes** | *makes* **about 1 gallon**

Meaty carcasses from 2 (4- to
   5-pound) roasted chickens
6 carrots, tops removed
1 small bunch celery
1 large brown-skinned onion
2 shallots
2 bay leaves
Handful parsley, chopped
Small handful fresh thyme sprigs

- Place the chicken carcasses in a large stockpot. Chop the carrots, celery, onion, and shallots into roughly 2-inch pieces, leaving any skins (including onion skin) on for color. Add them to the pot, along with the bay leaves, parsley, and thyme, and fill the pot almost to the top with water. Bring to a boil over high heat, then reduce to a bare simmer and cook, stirring every hour or so and working the chicken off the bones with a wooden spoon once or twice, for 5 hours.

- Remove the stock from the heat and let it cool for about an hour. Carefully pour it through a colander into a large bowl or two, then through a fine-mesh strainer into smaller freezable containers. (Make sure the stock isn't hot enough to melt the plastic.) Refrigerate the containers overnight, then skim off the fat, cover, label with the date, and freeze. Stock should last about 6 months in the freezer.

- To use, take the stock out of the freezer, run the container under warm water to release the sides, and melt the frozen stock over low heat in a saucepan.

NOTE: For easier measuring, stock can also be refrigerated overnight in the bowl, then skimmed and frozen in 1-cup portions in small zip-top bags. Lay the bags flat during freezing for easier storage.

BASIC FRENCH VINAIGRETTE

This is the vinaigrette I keep on hand for general use; toss butter lettuce with very thinly sliced radishes and cucumbers and chopped avocados, along with some of this dressing, for an unbeatable dinner salad. It also makes a great marinade for meats.

active time **5 minutes** | *makes* **about 1 cup**

1 tablespoon Dijon mustard
1 small shallot, very finely chopped (about 2 tablespoons)
¼ cup champagne vinegar
Kosher salt and freshly ground black pepper
½ cup extra-virgin olive oil
2 tablespoons canola oil

- In a medium bowl, whisk the Dijon, shallot, vinegar, and salt and pepper to taste until well blended. While whisking, drizzle in the olive oil, then the canola oil, and continue whisking until completely emulsified. Taste the vinaigrette for seasoning; you may want a little more oil, vinegar, salt, and/or pepper.

HERB-ROASTED RED POTATOES

The simplest of side dishes is often the most satisfying. Don't skimp on the oil here or the potatoes will stick to the pan.

Most woody herbs (see page 78) work well for this recipe, so use thyme, rosemary, oregano, marjoram, sage, or a combination of any of the above.

active time **5 minutes** | *makes* **4 servings**

1 pound golf ball–size red potatoes, halved
1 tablespoon olive oil
2 cloves garlic, finely chopped
2 teaspoons finely chopped fresh herbs
Kosher salt and freshly ground black pepper

- Preheat the oven to 425°F.

- Mix the potatoes, olive oil, garlic, and herbs in a bowl to blend, and season to taste with salt and pepper. Transfer them to an ovenproof dish large enough to hold them in a single layer (for example, an 8-by-8-inch ceramic pan) and roast them for about 30 minutes, or until the potatoes are browned in spots and tender inside. Serve hot.

SIMPLE SAUTÉED GREENS

It may seem basic, but many people avoid buying great greens like chard, spinach, and kale because they aren't sure how to cook them. This simple method can be used for most greens, but I love using a combination of them—the three used together here make great panfellows. For an aromatic accompaniment to an Asian-inspired meal, substitute a mixture of canola and sesame oil for the olive oil, and finish the dish with rice wine vinegar and a splash of soy sauce.

If you don't have a scale handy, you'll need about two generous handfuls of each type of chopped greens. (See page 78 for tips on how to cut them.)

active time **20 minutes** | *makes* **4 servings**

1 tablespoon extra-virgin olive oil
2 cloves garlic, finely chopped
Pinch of crushed red pepper flakes (optional)
¼ pound kale, rinsed, tough ribs removed, and chopped (about 2 packed cups chopped)
¼ pound white, red, or rainbow chard, rinsed, tough ribs removed, and chopped (about 2 packed cups chopped)
¼ pound spinach, rinsed and chopped (about 2 packed cups chopped)
Kosher salt and freshly ground black pepper
1½ tablespoons sherry or red wine vinegar, or freshly squeezed lemon juice
2 tablespoons water or broth

- In a large skillet, combine the oil, garlic, and red pepper flakes and warm over medium heat. When the garlic begins to sizzle vigorously, after about 1 minute, add the kale, chard, and spinach, and season to taste with salt and pepper. Cook, stirring often, until the greens are wilted, about 5 minutes. (If all the greens don't fit in your pan at the beginning, add them in batches as the first greens cook down.) Add the vinegar and water, and sauté for another minute or so, until most of the liquid has evaporated. Heap the greens into a small bowl and serve immediately.

SIMPLE MASHED SQUASH

Kabocha squash is naturally quite sweet, and when cooked, its flesh is silky, which makes it an ideal candidate for mashing. This mash will be thicker or thinner depending on how much liquid you add, so play with it. For a slightly different flavor, try adding ground cumin, curry powder, cardamom, or *pimentón de la Vera* (smoked Spanish paprika; see page 75 for where to purchase), or boost the dish's richness by adding cream, sour cream, yogurt, or crème fraîche in addition to the broth. Honey, brown sugar, or maple syrup are great accents as well.

active time **15 minutes** | *makes* **4 to 6 servings**

1 (3-pound) kabocha squash
½ teaspoon kosher salt
½ cup to 1 cup Homemade Chicken Stock (page 185), store-bought chicken or vegetable broth, or milk
2 to 4 tablespoons unsalted butter, cut into cubes (optional)

- Preheat the oven to 400°F. Halve the squash, scoop out the seeds, and place cut side up on a parchment- or aluminum foil–lined baking sheet. Bake until a fork enters the thickest part of the squash very easily, about an hour.

- When the squash is just cool enough to handle, use a serving spoon to scrape the flesh out of the skins, avoiding or slicing off any tough skin. Transfer the flesh to a food processor or blender, and whirl together with the salt, stock, and butter until extremely smooth. Taste for seasoning, adding more salt if necessary, adjust the texture with more liquid and/or butter, and serve warm.

NOTE: The squash can be made up to 3 days ahead. Cool it to room temperature, transfer it to a reheatable serving dish, and cover it with aluminum foil. To reheat, bake the squash for 20 minutes at 350°F, or transfer it to a soup pot and warm over low heat, stirring frequently.

SIMPLE ROASTED TOMATOES

In the fall in Seattle, when the idea of standing in front of the oven again is actually palatable, the Market is often still bursting with great tomatoes. Snuggle these into a bowl next to Braised Halibut with Caramelized Fennel and Olives (page 73) or One-Pan Coq Au Vin (page 169)—they all cook at the same temperature—chop them into a pasta sauce, or serve them atop simply grilled meats or fish. Add finely minced garlic in addition to the chopped garlic, if it's popular in your house.

active time **5 minutes** | *makes* **4 servings**

8 roma tomatoes, halved lengthwise
2 cloves garlic, smashed and roughly chopped
1 tablespoon extra-virgin olive oil
1 tablespoon chopped fresh oregano
Kosher salt and freshly ground black pepper

- Preheat the oven to 450°F.

- Mix the tomatoes, garlic, oil, and oregano together in a medium bowl. Transfer to an ovenproof baking dish and arrange the tomatoes in one layer, cut sides up. Season liberally with salt and pepper, and bake on the middle rack of the oven for 15 to 20 minutes, until soft. Serve immediately.

MENU SUGGESTIONS

Appetizers for a Crowd

Etta's Mini Dungeness Crab Cakes with Green Cocktail Sauce (page 7)
Deviled Duck Eggs with Green Olives, Smoked Paprika, and Fried Capers (page 88)
Spicy Marinated Feta (page 90)
Potato and Pea Samosas with Minted Yogurt Dipping Sauce (page 67)

Asian-Inspired Dinner

Hot-Sweet Mango Pickles (page 99)
Za'atar-Crusted Chicken with Harissa-Yogurt Sauce (page 100)
Berbere Chickpea and Carrot Tagine (page 93)

Book Club Lunch

Downtown Duck Salad (page 118)
MarketSpice Tea Cake (page 142)

Fall Market Feast

Carrot Soup with Cumin and Honey (page 75)
Mixed Greens with Basic French Vinaigrette (page 186)
Braised Hanging Tender with Wild Mushrooms, Rosemary, and Juniper (page 123)
Butternut Squash Bread Pudding (page 148)

Fast Summer Supper

Seared Salmon with Two-Cherry Relish (page 22)
Simple Roasted Tomatoes (page 190)
Simple Sautéed Greens (page 188)

French-Inspired Weeknight Dinner Party

Garlicky Goat Cheese Mousse (page 87)
One-Pan Coq Au Vin (page 169)
French-Style Apple Custard Cake (page 46)

Make-Ahead Sunday Picnic

Three Greens Tart with Goat Cheese and Pine Nuts (page 66)
Greek Chicken Salad (page 113)
Mediterranean Pasta Salad with Seven-Grain Orzo (page 95)
Tart Cherry Chocolate Chunk Oatmeal Cookies (page 50)

Rainy-Day Lunch

Pike Place Chowder's Market Chowder (page 12)
Outrageous Garlic Breadsticks (page 183)
Lavender Shortbread (page 146)

Show-Off Dinner

Elderflower Champagne Cocktail (page 176)
Il Bistro's Guido Contini (page 163)
Scotch-Spiked Chicken Liver Pâté (page 166)
Salade Verte (page 58)
Orecchiette Pasta with Cauliflower Cream and Shaved Black Truffles (page 96)
Spiced Apricot Tarte Tatin (page 48)

Spring Celebration

Brie with Sautéed Chanterelles (made with morel mushrooms) (page 38)
Roast Leg of Lamb with Garlicky Nettle Pesto (page 126)
Roasted Pancetta-Wrapped Asparagus with Goat Cheese (page 74)
Herb-Roasted Red Potatoes (page 184)

Summer Backyard Barbecue

Three Girls' Gazpacho (page 61)
Blackened Salmon Sandwiches (page 15)
Nectarine, Blueberry, and Candied Hazelnut Crisp (page 150)

Sunday Brunch

Seatown Pickled King Salmon with Horseradish Cream (page 9)
Spring Frittata with Morels, Asparagus, Peas, and Ramps (page 36)
Honey Cream Biscuits (page 86)
Simple Roasted Tomatoes (page 190)
Etta's Scratch Bloody Mary with Pickled Carrots (page 161)

Vegetarian (But No One Will Notice)

Mexican-Spiced Sopaipillas (page 92)
Alex's Vegetable Chili (page 69)
Fran's Gold Bar Brownies (page 144)

A Visit to Italy

Shredded White Winter Salad with Endive, Pears, and Blue Cheese (page 40)
Linguine alla Vongole (page 170)
Classic Biscotti with Vin Santo (page 177)

Winter Warmer

Roasted Pickled Cauliflower Salad (page 62)
Beer-Braised Brisket with Glazed Carrots and Parsnips (page 172)
Simple Mashed Squash (page 189)

RESOURCES

Although some of the Pike Place Market's goods can be replaced by similar substitutes, many of the recipes in this book call for ingredients made only right in (or around) the Market. For more information about shipping foods used in a certain recipe or to try the original version of a dish in this book, contact or visit the purveyors listed here. Some in the list below offer both ingredients and prepared food; some offer just one or the other. All are worth a stop.

Denotes a business outside the Pike Place Market Historic District.

Shops and Quick Stops

ATHENIAN INN SEAFOOD RESTAURANT AND BAR
1517 Pike Place / Main Arcade
(206) 624-7166 / athenianinn.com

BAVARIAN MEATS DELICATESSEN
1920 Pike Place / Pike Place–Soames-Dunn Building
(206) 441-0942 / bavarianmeats.com

BEECHER'S HANDMADE CHEESE
1600 Pike Place / Pike Place–North End at Pine Street
(206) 956-1964 / beechershandmadecheese.com

CHOICE PRODUCE & PEPPER
1514 Pike Place #4 / Sanitary Market Building
(206) 623-9920 / choicepeppers.com

CHUKAR CHERRIES
1529B Pike Place / Main Arcade
(206) 623-8043 / chukar.com

CINNAMON WORKS
1536 Pike Place / Triangle Building
(206) 583-0085 / cinnamonworks.com

CITY FISH
1535 Pike Place / North Arcade
(800) 334-2669 / cityfish.com

THE CONFECTIONAL
1530 Pike Place / Triangle Building
(206) 282-4422 / theconfectional.com

THE CRUMPET SHOP
1503 First Avenue / Corner Market Building
(206) 682-1598

DAILY DOZEN DOUGHNUT COMPANY
93 Pike Street #7 / Economy Market Building
(206) 467-7769

DELAURENTI SPECIALTY FOOD & WINE
1435 First Avenue / Economy Market Building
(206) 622-0141 / delaurenti.com

DON AND JOE'S MEATS
85 Pike Street / La Salle Building
(206) 682-7670 / donandjoesmeats.com

EL MERCADO LATINO
1514 Pike Place #6 / Sanitary Market Building
(206) 623-3240 / latinmerchant.com

FRANK'S QUALITY PRODUCE
1508 Pike Place / Corner Market Building
(206) 624-5666 / franksproduce.net

*FRAN'S CHOCOLATES
1325 First Avenue
(206) 682-0168 / franschocolates.com

HOLMQUIST HAZELNUT ORCHARDS
Pike Place–North Arcade
(800) 720-0895 / holmquisthazelnuts.com

I LOVE NEW YORK DELI
93 Pike Street #4 / Economy Market Building
(206) 381-3354 / ilovenewyorkdeli.net

*IL CORVO
1501 Western Avenue, Suite 300
(206) 622-4280 / ilcorvopasta.wordpress.com

JACK'S FISH SPOT
1514 Pike Place / Sanitary Market Building
(206) 467-0514 / jacksfishspot.com

LA BUONA TAVOLA TRUFFLE CAFÉ AND SPECIALTY FOODS
1524 Pike Place / Triangle Building
(206) 292-5555 / trufflecafe.com

LE PANIER
1902 Pike Place / Pike Place–North End at Stewart Street
(206) 441-3669 / lepanier.com

MARKET CELLAR WINERY
1432 Western Avenue
(206) 622-1880 / marketcellarwinery.com

MARKET GRILL
1509 Pike Place #3 / Main Arcade
(206) 682-2654

MARKETSPICE
85A Pike Place / La Salle Building
(206) 622-6340 / marketspice.com

MARTIN FAMILY ORCHARDS
1501 Pike Place / North Arcade and Pike Place
(509) 784-1700

MEE SUM PASTRY
1533 Pike Place / Triangle Building
(206) 682-6780 / meesum.com

MEXICAN GROCERY
1914 Pike Place / Pike Place–Soames-Dunn Building
(206) 441-1147

MOON VALLEY HONEY
1903 Pike Place #A / North Arcade
(206) 623-0158 / moonvalleyhoney.com

MR. D'S GREEK DELICACIES
1518 Pike Place / Triangle Building
(206) 622-4881 / mrdsgreekdelicacies.netfirms.com

ORIENTAL MART
1506 Pike Place #509 / Corner Market Building
(206) 622-8488

PAPPARDELLE'S PASTA
1519 Pike Place #8 / Main Arcade
(206) 340-4114 / pappardellesonline.com

*PATTERSON CELLARS
1427 Western Avenue
(206) 724-0664 / pattersoncellars.com

PEAR DELICATESSEN & SHOPPE
1926 Pike Place / Pike Place–Champion Building
(206) 443-1926 / pearatpikeplace.com

PIKE PLACE BAKERY
1501 Pike Place / Main Arcade
(206) 682-2829 / pikeplacebakery.com

PIKE PLACE CHINESE CUISINE
1533 Pike Place / DownUnder (Level 4)
(206) 223-0292 / pikeplacechinesecuisine.com

PIKE PLACE CHOWDER
1530 Post Alley / Post Alley Market
(206) 267-2537 / pikeplacechowder.com

PIKE PLACE FISH
86 Pike Place / Main Arcade
(800) 542-7732 / pikeplacefish.com

PIKE PLACE MARKET CREAMERY
1514 Pike Place #3 / Sanitary Market Building
(206) 622-5029

PIKE PLACE NUTS
97-A Pike St. #2 / Economy Market Building
(206) 623-8204 / pikeplacenuts.com

*PIKE BREWING COMPANY
1415 First Avenue
(206) 622-6044 / pikebrewing.com

PIKE & WESTERN WINE SHOP
1934 Pike Place
(206) 441-1307 / pikeandwestern.com

PIROSHKY PIROSHKY
1908 Pike Place / Pike Place–Stewart House
(206) 441-6068 / piroshkybakery.com

PURE FOOD FISH MARKET
1511 Pike Place / Main Arcade
(800) 392-3474 / freshseafood.com

QUALITY CHEESE
1508 Pike Place / Sanitary Market Building
(206) 624-4029

SAFFRON SPICE
93 Pike Street #3 / Economy Market Building
(206) 682-2593 / saffronspice.weebly.com

SOSIO'S FRUIT & PRODUCE
1527 Pike Place / Main Arcade
(206) 622-1370

SOTTO VOCE
1532 Pike Place / Triangle Building
(206) 624-9998 / sottovoce.com

THE SOUK
1916 Pike Place #11 / Pike Place–Soames-Dunn Building
(206) 441-1666

THE SPANISH TABLE
1426 Western Avenue
(206) 682-2827 / spanishtable.com

STARBUCKS COFFEE COMPANY
1912 Pike Place / Pike Place–Soames-Dunn Building
(206) 448-8762 / starbucks.com

SUR LA TABLE
84 Pine Street
(206) 448-2244 / surlatable.com

THE TASTING ROOM
1924 Post Alley / Upper Post Alley
(206) 770-9463 / thetastingroom.com

THREE GIRLS BAKERY
1514 Pike Place, Suite 1 / Sanitary Market Building
(206) 622-1045

TINY'S ORGANIC
On Pike Place
(206) 850-3467 / tinysorganic.com

TOTEM SMOKEHOUSE
1906 Pike Place, Suite 1 / Pike Place–Stewart House
(800) 972-5666 / totemsmokehouse.com

ULI'S FAMOUS SAUSAGE
1511 Pike Place / Main Arcade
(206) 839-1000 / ulisfamoussausage.com

WOODRING NORTHWEST
1529 Pike Place / Main Arcade
(206) 340-2705 / woodringnorthwest.com

*WORLD SPICE
1509 Western Avenue
(206) 682-7274 / worldspice.com

Restaurants
·····················

You could eat at the Pike Place Market all day, every day, for a month and still not have the same thing twice. Here are the fancier restaurants featured in this book; reservations are recommended.

*ART RESTAURANT & LOUNGE
99 Union Street
(206) 749-7070 / artrestaurantseattle.com

CAFÉ CAMPAGNE
1600 Post Alley
(206) 728-2233 / cafecampagne.com

*ETTA'S
2020 Western Avenue
(206) 443-6000 / tomdouglas.com

*LECOSHO
89 University Street / Lower Post Alley
(206) 623-2101 / lecosho.com

LE PICHET
1933 First Avenue
(206) 256-1499 / lepichetseattle.com

MARCHÉ
86 Pine Street / Inn at the Market
(206) 728-2800 / marcheseattle.com

MATT'S IN THE MARKET
94 Pike Street, Suite 32 / Corner Market Building
(206) 467-7909 / mattsinthemarket.com

MAXIMILIEN RESTAURANT
81-A Pike Street / LaSalle Building
(206) 682-7270 / maximilienrestaurant.com

THE PINK DOOR
1919 Post Alley / Upper Post Alley
(206) 443-3241 / thepinkdoor.net

*SEATOWN SEABAR & ROTISSERIE
2010 Western Avenue
(206) 436-0390 / tomdouglas.com

STEELHEAD DINER
95 Pine Street / Post Alley Market
(206) 625-0129 / steelheaddiner.com

*THOA'S RESTAURANT & LOUNGE
96 Union Street
(206) 344-8088 / thoaseattle.com

Other

PIKE PLACE MARKET
pikeplacemarket.org

SAVOR SEATTLE FOOD TOURS
savorseattletours.com

ACKNOWLEDGMENTS

Making a book requires a huge number of participants, especially when the book—like *Pike Place Market Recipes*—is about a place with so many moving parts and so many wonderful, spirited, animated, hard-working people. I'd shout my thank-yous from the top of the Market sign, if I was allowed, but I'm afraid I might not be heard over its current earthquake retrofitting project.

The Market's purveyors, shop owners, chefs, and restaurateurs were crucial to writing this book, and it must be noted first and foremost that they donated their time and recipes graciously and voluntarily. I'd also like to thank the Market's Preservation and Development Authority, which oversees the use of the Pike Place Market's trademarks and helped me research the book.

Thanks to Gary Luke and the entire editing and design team at Sasquatch Books, who encouraged me to write *Pike Place Market Recipes*, and to Clare Barboza, the photographer extraordinaire who made this book so beautiful. (Clare, I never expected to laugh so hard.)

Thanks to Carroll Pierce, a former client from my private cheffing days in Woods Hole, Massachusetts, for being the first person to tell me I should be writing cookbooks, and for testing and retesting far beyond the call of duty. Thanks to Hilary Halttunen, for running to the store with three kids under five at 5:30 p.m. on a weeknight for eggs, convincing her husband they'd made a dash for the hospital because she left her phone on the counter, the oven and television on, and dinner halfway cooked. Thanks to Mary Russell, who battled chemotherapy nausea to cook for her family when food was the farthest thing from her mind. And thanks to all my other fabulous testers: Sarah Collyer, Laura Russell, Lauren Bedford, Claire Horner-Devine, Katy Leach, Dierk Yochim, Dana Wootton, Tami Horner, Erica Howe, and my moms, Amy Howe and Nancy Thomson. Special thanks to my readers, Rebekah Denn and Alida Moore, for dealing with me when sanity faltered, and to Vicki Moen, Dan Horner, Joe Talbert, Hannah Viano, and Allison Howe, for always being hungry.

Deepest appreciation goes to Kathy Gunst, who taught me to write recipes and love doing it; to my husband, Jim, for doing more dishes each month than any person should do in a lifetime; and to our son, Graham. When I most needed it, he learned to say, "It's good."

INDEX

Note: Photographs are indicated by *italics*.

ABOUT THE AUTHOR

Jess Thomson is a Seattle-based freelance writer and cookbook author. Her work has appeared in such publications as *Sunset, Food & Wine, Cooking Light, Edible Seattle,* and *Seattle Metropolitan* magazines. She is a contributor at *Leite's Culinaria,* where her work was chosen for inclusion in *Best Food Writing 2008* and *2010.* She was also a finalist for a Bert Greene Award for food journalism in 2009. Jess, a graduate of Middlebury College and The Cambridge School of Culinary Arts, is the author of the food blog *hogwash* (www.jessthomson.wordpress .com), where she pairs food and life. She is also the author of *Top Pot Hand-Forged Doughnuts: Secrets and Recipes for the Home Baker.*

About the Photographer

Clare Barboza is a Seattle-based food photographer, with a passion for documenting how food goes from the farm to the kitchen to the table. She has photographed several cookbooks and regularly shoots for various publications, restaurants, and chefs. She also leads a variety of photography workshops out of her studio in downtown Seattle.